THE GLOBE-TROTTING
GOLFER'S GUIDE TO RETIREMENT

DAVE D'ANTONI

ISBN: 1453886648
ISBN-13: 9781453886649
LCCN: 2010915599

Library of Congress Control Number: 2010915599

FOREWORD

*I have always believed it was easier to learn
from the mistakes of others. I only wish I could have
been better at actually doing it.*

— *Dave*

In October 2004, at age 59 years, eight months and 20 days, I retired to begin enjoying the rest of my life. Along the way, I've made some mistakes and have learned a lot about the challenges and opportunities of retirement. What I've learned, including from my errors, is what this book is all about. I hope that it will help you avoid some of the problems that many people encounter and get the key retirement decisions right the first time, so that you, too, can truly enjoy and make the most of your retirement years – to make that last third or more of your life the very best third.

Not that I hadn't enjoyed the previous six decades. I'd grown up in Huntington, West Virginia, the eldest son of the owner of a sporting goods store and a wonderful, stay-at-home mother. They had met at Marshall University, where my dad had been the quarterback on the school's very successful football team. My parents loved golf and played it well into their eighties. I'm fortunate that they are both still active today.

In 1967 I received my bachelor's degree in chemical engineering from Virginia Tech. A week after graduation, I married Sue Ann Totten in Marmet, West Virginia. Sue Ann and I are still happily married with a daughter, Jennifer; a son, Andy; and a miniature dachshund, Rudy.

I spent almost all my career in the chemical industry, starting as a process engineer and reaching senior vice president by the time I retired. I loved my job (most of the time); but for me, work was not the end in itself; it was the means to an end.

I have now been happily and busily retired for just over six and a half years. It's hard for me to believe that the time has gone by so fast. During that time, Sue Ann and I have moved to our second home in Florida and sold our Ohio home of 25 years, after first selling all the furniture and fixtures at a tag sale. This wasn't easy for us or for our now-grown children, since we'd all loved that house.

Also in these six and a half years, I have played more than 1500 rounds of golf, with the result that my handicap has dropped from nine to four. Trips with the guys have accounted for about 100 of these rounds, half of them in Scotland, Ireland, Spain and Mexico.

My wife and I have taken 13 major trips, as well. We've toured China, Hawaii, Scandinavia, Italy, Spain, Greece, Hungary, Germany, Austria, the Netherlands, Portugal and a few other countries. We've cruised on small, medium and large ships and on riverboats. We've been on many, many land tours by bus and even one on a high-speed train.

Because I worked for a well-managed company in a growing industry that recognized the value of its engineers and executives and compensated us well, and because my wife and I began planning for retirement early in my career, we are now able to enjoy a high standard of living. However, the lessons I've learned apply whatever your means. Designing a good retirement for yourself and your spouse is not just a matter of being financially ready or picking the right place to live or electing good medical care or finding the most compatible friends or deciding how you want to spend your time. It's about all of these and more.

From the time I started my first real job after graduating from college, I've always been fascinated by why people retired and what they did afterwards. I observed that retirement didn't guarantee a long life – or a happy one. I found that many people struggled with retirement. Some hated it, and many people completely "flunked" it.

On the other hand, many were able to have a long, healthy and happy retirement. So what was the difference? I asked both successful and failed retirees about their experiences and what they considered the reasons for their success or failure. After awhile, I began to see a pattern of decisions and actions that led to a satisfying retirement. In my late forties,

I began planning for my own retirement using these guidelines.

During the six and a half years since I retired myself, I've observed even more retirees. Some of them haven't been very happy, but others have been happy, healthy and fulfilled. I've learned that retirement isn't easy. It is not sitting around. It requires lots of thought and planning. You have to know what you truly want to do, what you like to do and what you want no part of.

Retirement isn't all about you. In fact, if you're half of a couple, it may not even be primarily about you. (This was a big lesson for me.)

Once I retired, I began to get questions about retirement from friends and acquaintances who were still working. Some of them had planned ahead; unfortunately, even more had no clue about how to approach retirement's challenges and opportunities.

In 2008 I was discussing my thoughts on retirement with a colleague, Tom Markert. He listened intently and responded that everyone over 40 needed this information, even young people just starting their careers and people who've already retired. He said, "You have a book here."

I figured that Tom was correct. After all, he himself is the author of two books: *You Can't Win a Fight with Your Boss* (published in India as *100 Rules for Career Success*) and *You Can't Win a Fight with Your Client*. In exchange for my advice on retirement, Tom gave me advice on book-writing, plus a lot of encouragement.

Thank you, Tom. I have truly enjoyed getting my thoughts together.

Finally, I could not have completed with book or gotten it published without the wonderful help and encouragement of Sandy Sheehy. Sandy was very helpful in organizing and structuring my thoughts and leading the effort to get the book published. Sandy is an author in her own right. She has written *Connecting: The Enduring Power of Female Friendship* and *Texas Big Rich*. Many thanks to you, Sandy.

So here we go.

Dave D'Antoni
Naples, Florida
March 31, 2011

TABLE OF CONTENTS

Foreword   1
Introduction   9

Section One: Pre-Retirement Planning   13
Chapter 1   The Value of Your Retirement Years   15
Chapter 2   Get Your Body Ready   23
Chapter 3   Early Planning   27
Chapter 4   The Spouse   33
Chapter 5   Financial Preparation   39
Chapter 6   Getting Started   49
Chapter 7   Where and When   53
Chapter 8   Location   57
Chapter 9   A House, a Condo, a Home   65
Chapter 10 A Great Community   71

Section Two: The First Days of the Rest of Your Life   75
Chapter 11 Retirement, Day One   77
Chapter 12 The Spouse in Retirement   81
Chapter 13 Job One: Staying Alive   87
Chapter 14 Managing Your Calendar   93
Chapter 15 Guests and Visitors   97
Chapter 16 Get Involved with People   101
Chapter 17 Stay Flexible Financially   105
Chapter 18 How Did We Get So Old?   111
Chapter 19 Live the Dream!   115

Section Three: Golf: My Key to a Successful Retirement   119
Chapter 20 "But What If I Don't Like Golf?"   121
Chapter 21 What's So Great about Golf?   127

Chapter 22 Put Another Way:
            My Favorite Golf Quotations   133
Chapter 23 Joining a Golf Club   137
Chapter 24 The Joy of New Clubs   143
Chapter 25 The Unwritten Rules of Golf   147
Chapter 26 Couples Golf   151
Chapter 27 Traveling with Your Golf Group   153
Chapter 28 Rules for a Golf Trip Competition 159

Section Four: Travel: The Other Reason to Retire 165
Chapter 29 Where in the World Should we Go?   167
Chapter 30 Start Way before Retiring   171
Chapter 31 Travel Tips   175
Chapter 32 Making the Most of Cruising   183
Chapter 33 The Caribbean   191
Chapter 34 The Mediterranean   197
Chapter 35 Alaska   219
Chapter 36 Scandinavian Capitals   227
Chapter 37 River Cruises   237
Chapter 38 Land-Based Tours   245
Chapter 39 China   259
Chapter 40 Safaris   265
Chapter 41 Hawaii: The Joy of Staying Put   273
Chapter 42 Looking Ahead   281

INTRODUCTION

*Retirement is worth working hard for and when
achieved, is too valuable to waste even a little of it.*

— *Dave*

Retirement can be a wonderful time. It certainly is for me – time for golf, world travel, neighborhood parties, and dinners with friends, at home or out. Every night is Saturday night.

But as anyone can attest who lived through the sub-prime mortgage meltdown and stock market crash of 2008 and the subsequent recession, the landscape can shift almost overnight. Many people who retired thinking that their stock dividends and mutual funds would support their lifestyles found that they had to sell some assets, including second or third homes. Others had to go back to work. People who thought their pensions were secure suddenly had to face the prospect of their former employers declaring bankruptcy. And even relatively fortunate retirees found that they needed to cut back on spending and conserve what money they'd accumulated.

Obviously, the financial crisis affected not only those already retired; it also affected the millions of Baby Boomers who were about to retire. It is this group that I think can benefit most from this book.

None of us knows just how long we will live. Our genes and our lifestyles, everything from accidents of birth to accidents on the highway, can result in our having more or less time remaining than the actuarial tables show for people born in our birth year. But one thing we do know is that our life expectancy is limited. The longer we work, the shorter our time in retirement. And if we wait until the deterioration of our health forces us to bow out of the workplace, we will have spent all of our precious years of vigorous health and mobility at the office, rather than focusing on the activities and relationships we enjoy most.

For those who delay retirement, whether out of financial necessity or out of the meaning and affirmation they derive from their jobs, it is especially important to plan well for retirement. They, even more than others, need to understand the decisions that must be made early, to take them seriously and make them well, so that the day work stops, retirement starts, without any wasted time, energy or money. They need to know what they will do and where they will do it and to be physically, financially and emotionally able to do it before they walk out the office door for the last time.

In addition, there are many things you can begin doing while you are still working to sample the retirement life right now, as you lay the groundwork for a satisfying retirement in the future.

That's why this little book is divided into four sections. Section One covers retirement advice for anyone, whatever his or her interests. Section Two deals with the transition from working stiff to happy retiree. (It's not as easy as it sounds.) Whatever your interests, if you're over 50, this is for you. Section Three is devoted to enjoying my favorite sport, golf, which I consider reason enough for retirement. Section Four addresses another of my passions (and another argument for early retirement), travel.

If you prefer tennis or fishing to golf and can only sleep well in your own bed, you can skip Sections Three and Four; but whatever your interests, pay close attention to Sections One and Two. They could change the rest of your life, and your spouse's – for the better.

SECTION ONE

PRE-RETIREMENT PLANNING

Never put off until tomorrow what you can do today!
— my mother, among others

CHAPTER 1

THE VALUE OF YOUR RETIREMENT YEARS

My plan is to live forever..... So far, so good.
— Dave

If you are currently employed, no matter how much you love your job, no matter how much you enjoy your colleagues, no matter how much affirmation you reap from being part of the team or contributing your skills to society, unless you die at your desk (literally or figuratively), the time will come when you will retire. And like anything else in life, your retirement will go much better if you invest the thought in it that you would invest in any other important aspect of life. It certainly deserves as much planning as a career change, and maybe even as much as deciding when you want to begin your family and how many children you want to have.

The best time to start planning for your retirement is while you're approaching the peak of your career – in your forties or even in your late thirties. In fact, the twenties aren't too early, when you're embarking on your first "real" job. But even if you're in your early sixties, or have already retired, retirement planning can be very productive. (If you're at that stage, read this book and then pass it along to your kids.)

Thinking about retirement begins with recognizing the VALUE of each retirement year.

There are at least two indisputable facts that must be considered when thinking about this concept:

1. Your retirement will end at your death.

Some people might say that since 100% of divorced people were married, marriage must be the cause of divorce. We know that this isn't the case. However, it is true that marriage is a prerequisite for divorce. Likewise, retirement does not cause death. In fact, unfortunately many people die before they retire (or before they can truly enjoy retirement). What a shame and what a waste of an opportunity!

Death and taxes, as they say, are inevitable for all of us. That means that the years we spend in retirement are limited, and therefore precious.

2. Retirement years are usually divided into three phases.

So we know what the end to our retirement will be. What takes understanding and planning is the time in between work and death.

For much of the twentieth century, medical and social scientists looked at the years beyond age 65 as a block. Whatever gentler phrase they may have used, it was Old Age. But more recent thinking recognizes that there's a world of difference between 66 and 86, and between 86 and 96. And as the average life expectancy grows longer, those differences become even more apparent. Researchers are still struggling with where to set and what to call the sub-stages of later life that these differences define, but for ease of discussion, I'll divide them as follows:

1. The Active Years

2. The Middle Years

3. The Declining Years

As the name implies, the Active Years are the years when you will be able to do all the same things that you have always been able to do. You will be able to travel and participate in sports or other activities. Most folks are actually in better condition during this period than they were while they were still working, because they have the time to be much more active. According to the U.S. Department of Health and Human Services report titled *Health, United States, 2008*, only 9% of U.S. adults will face a limitation on activities due to heart problems and only 12% will be limited by arthritis during the years between 65 and 74.

The Middle Years are the years when things become a little more difficult. Joints begin to ache and may need to be replaced. Physical strength, flexibility and stamina begin to decline. Reflexes are not what they used to be. People can still be very active during this phase, but it gets more difficult and perhaps more painful. According to the report above, during the years between 75 and 84, 15% and 17% of

U.S. adults will face limitations due to heart problems and arthritis, respectively.

The Declining Years are the years when mobility decreases sharply and physical activity becomes very difficult. Serious problems begin to occur not only with joints but now with organs and perhaps memory. Over age 85, the percentage of Americans who will face limitations because of heart problems and arthritis is estimated to be 21% and 27%, respectively. And we all know how the Declining Years phase ends. None of us wants to think about the Declining Years. We can only hope that they will last a short period of time and not be too unpleasant or too expensive.

There are no set ages for these three stages. Some people require hip replacements in their sixties; others are still running marathons in their eighties. I am very fortunate that my family seems to be blessed with longevity. Both of my parents are still alive and well at 93 and 89. Although they are healthy and active, they are clearly well into the Middle Years of retirement.

My mother and father still live on their own and enjoy being able to drive, play card games such as bridge and gin, go to parties and entertain their friends. However, their Active Years of traveling and playing golf are past.

Thus, the primary objective of retirement is to extend and maximize the value of your Active Years. While this objective is hard to dispute, to implement an effective plan for extending and maximizing your Active Years, you need to estimate how many you will likely have.

The number of Active Years will be different for each individual; but as an engineer by training, I know that it can be helpful to make an estimate of how many Active Years you might have available.

According to *Health, United States, 2008* prepared by the U.S. Department of Health and Human Services, life expectancies for 65-year-old men and women in the United States in 2005, the latest data available, were 82 and 85 years respectively. The good news is that both these averages had increased about one year since 2000. The bad news is that these are averages, meaning that you may have more years or fewer; and these life expectancies include all of the three phases of the rest of your life.

If you are a man and start with the assumptions that you will live to the average life expectancy and will retire at age 65, you can expect to live 17.2 more years; if you are a woman, 20 more years. As a somewhat educated guess, based on my personal observations, you might assume a 40%, 40%, 20% split for the Active Years, the Middle Years, and the Declining Years, respectively.

Based on these assumptions, a man's Active Years and Middle Years would last about seven years each. Based on this math, your Active Years would end at about age 72. The mathematical implications of this are that *each* of the years between 65 and 72

QUALITY OF LIFE

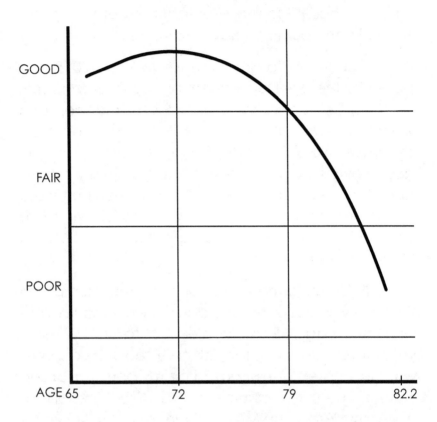

would represent about 14% of your total Active Years. Another way to look at this is that your Active Years become increasingly more valuable as time moves on, as shown in the table below.

AGE YEAR	VALUE OF A YEAR BASED ON THE PERCENT OF ACTIVE YEARS
65	14%
66	17%
67	20%
68	25%
69	33%
70	50%
71	100%

The way to read this is that your 65th year, with six more Active Years remaining, represents 14% of your remaining Active Years. While your 69th year with only three more Active Years remaining, is one third of the Active Years that remain. Years get much more valuable as time goes on, because fewer of them remain. This important concept is the basis for much of what follows.

The simple point of all of this is that after age 65, there is a relatively short period of time when you will be able to enjoy a fully active lifestyle. These will be the best years of the rest of your life and should not be wasted.

The most obvious way to increase the number of your Active Years in retirement is simply to retire before age 65 if you can. Retiring at 60 instead of at 65 will increase your theoretical Active Years from seven to twelve years, a 70% increase!

Other ways to extent this important period are discussed in Chapter 2.

Each of us has a different life expectancy. It depends on the genes that we inherit from our family, our lifestyle choices, and to some extent luck in not getting hit by the proverbial beer truck. I suggest that you use this simple model to make your own estimate of the number of your likely Active Years, because this concept should be the basis for many of the key decisions that you will need to make as you plan and enter your retirement years.

Since retirement, my wife and I have been very active – a lifestyle I highly recommend. Both of us have played a lot of golf and traveled extensively. Our observations of others are that most people who remain active, or even who take up the active life-style in retirement, are in good shape (Active Years) into their early seventies. Many are in great shape for much longer. But as it is often said, "All good things must come to an end."

The Middle Years are not the end, but they do represent a major change in lifestyle for most folks. You may be able walk or swim but may not be able to run or play tennis, for example. You may be able to take your grandchildren to the zoo but not white-water rafting. You may be able to take a plane to see your grandchildren but need to ride one of those annoying beeping carts to your gate. You may get together with your buddies for poker or to watch a bowl game but not so often for golf or hunting.

Much of this timing is out of our control, but there are a few simple things that we can do to make the most of and possibly extend the number of Active Years that we have. That is what the next chapter of this book is all about.

CHAPTER 2

GET YOUR BODY READY

Retirement is not about sitting around.
If done correctly, it requires a lot of energy.

— *Dave*

It is obvious that to have a long and enjoyable retirement, you have to stay alive and healthy. Even more importantly, you have to stay mobile. And you have to prepare yourself to avoid chronic diseases, such as diabetes, and if you do develop them, to prevent their most debilitating complications, and to fight life-threatening diseases, like cancer, with all of your resources and with a positive attitude.

My good friend John Reiner was diagnosed with stage four colon/liver cancer in his fifties but battled his disease into remission, even though the world-renowned Cleveland Clinic gave him only a 1% chance of survival. John fought. Reading everything he could find by people who had survived advanced cancer, he took charge of his own treatment and tried everything. He meditated. He became a temporary vegan. He avoided aluminum cookware and consumed only unusual foods and drink, including lots of combined carrot and celery juice. He beat it! His favorite saying now is "Staying alive is very hard work." He describes his program in what he calls "The Protocol." You can access John's protocol from my web site www.the-golobetrottinggolfer.com. Unfortunately, I lost two other friends to cancer very early in their retirement. We just don't know what our fate will be and how much time we have left.

Anyone can develop a serious health issue at any time. Some of this apparently is the result of our genetic heritage, and some is probably just bad luck. But most debilitating diseases are caused, at least in part, by the lifestyle choices that we have made.

There are many things we can and should do proactively to protect our health. You don't need to wait for retirement to get started. If you are not working on your health at this point, get started *now*!

There is a terrific book on this topic titled *Younger Next Year* by Chris Crowley and Henry S. Lodge, M.D. In this book, Crowley and Lodge persuasively make the case that you can delay the aging process and eliminate serious illnesses and injuries by working out regularly and not eating the wrong foods. I strongly recommend reading this book.

Retirement can offer many years of enjoyable activities, but most of these require good mobility. Tennis, golf, softball, dancing, hiking, walking, bicycling and even croquet demand the ability to get around. Mobility is also very important for enjoying travel, which is an important part of retirement for my wife and me. We have visited places and seen things that we were only able to imagine as we were growing up. Most of these experiences would have been impossible or at best difficult if we'd lacked mobility.

Long-term mobility is a function of joint health. In many cases, joint health is a function of body weight. I believe that excess weight is the biggest controllable threat to shortening the enjoyment of your valuable Active Years and probably your lifespan.

Some folks argue that their weight is not controllable. They say, and maybe even believe, that they have large bones, a family predisposition to put on pounds or a "set point" problem – a tendency to return, despite diet and exercise, to a certain percentage of body fat, which varies from one individual to another. I know because I mainly used the second reason for my obesity.

Luckily for me, as I was about to retire, my doctor told me, "Well, you have finally done it."

"What have I done?" I quickly asked.

"You have become pre-diabetic," he said.

"What does that mean?"

"It means that if you don't lose a bunch of weight and keep the weight off, you will soon be giving yourself insulin shots. Then in a few years we will have to cut your legs off," he said bluntly.

Believe me, he had my attention.

My doctor recommended a two-hour-a-week, four-week diabetes education program at our local hospital. This exceptionally well-presented program taught me about the disease, the medications available and the value of eating correctly and exercising.

I changed my eating habits immediately and began to drop weight. I had taken off pounds by dieting several times before, but this time it was not a diet; it was a permanent change in lifestyle. One of my great loves was cookies, especially during those long and often boring meetings I used to attend while working. It is now very easy for me to pass on cookies (and other sweets) by asking myself, "Would I rather have the cookies or my legs?"

If you currently have some health or joint issues and you are still working, take care of them before you retire. Get you teeth fixed; have a hip or knee replacement if needed. You do not want to waste any of your Active Years rehabilitating. If you are not exercising regularly, get started today to begin to build your strength and stamina.

Retirement can and should be a much more active lifestyle than your work life. Just imagine a week with seven weekend days instead of just two.

Get ready now!!!!

CHAPTER 3

EARLY PLANNING

Every move we make is calculated,
even the ones that aren't.

— Lisa's dad

Retirement takes a great amount of thought, planning and decision-making. As Lisa's dad told her, not making a decision will have its own results.

There are many choices that need to be thought through and decided. More than likely, you will not get all the decisions right the first time. Sue Ann and I didn't. In some areas there are no bad choices; but in others, a bad choice can either be extremely costly or, worse, irreversible. That's why making as many correct retirement choices as possible is very important.

I once asked a former executive from General Motors at what age he retired. "At 60," he said. I next asked him why he decided to retire early at 60. His response was very interesting, "Because I could not afford to retire at 55." He was a happy example of the principle that retiring early is the best way to extend your Active Years.

Thinking about retirement begins with answering two key questions:

"Who and what are most important to me?"

"What do I really want to do with the rest of my life?"

We have all heard that "I wish I had spent more time in the office" does not appear on anyone's tombstone. Interestingly, I do know folks who want to work well into their seventies (mainly lawyers, for some reason). Thankfully, that did not apply to me.

About 30 years ago I completed a very simple exercise at a training program provided by my employer. That exercise literally changed my life. It consists of making a table on a piece of paper. You start by listing yourself and everyone who is close or important to you in a column on the left side of the page. My list included myself, my wife, my children, my parents, my sisters and their spouses and children and a few very close friends.

The next column heading is "Current Ages," where you simply enter the current age for each person in the first column opposite his or her name. The following columns are headed "Plus 5 years," "Plus 10 years," "Plus 15 years," etc. The subsequent step is to extend the age for each person across the page in five-year increments.

When I completed this exercise many years ago, I recognized that we only had a few years left before our two kids left home and that my parents were nearing the end of their Active Years.

As a result of this simple exercise, Sue Ann and I began taking spring break trips with our children to different locations until they finished high school. We also took my parents with us to Hawaii a couple of times to enjoy the islands and play golf.

Without the insight from this simple exercise, my guess is that time would have passed in our busy lives, and we would have missed the opportunity to enjoy those fabulous experiences together as a family.

I highly recommend completing this exercise as you begin to think about retirement. In fact, I suggest you take 30 minutes and complete this exercise now. You will be amazed at what it will tell you.

Retirement years are about a lot more than you and your spouse. The situations of those around you will change with time. Kids, you hope, will graduate, leave home and become self sufficient. (You can never count on the last step actually happening, it seems.) Weddings will require funding. If you are blessed, grandchildren will arrive to be spoiled and educated. And your parents will be lost, perhaps after long and expensive stays in health care facilities.

As I started my retirement planning in my forties, I began asking questions of those who I knew who were retiring from my company. I asked my parents and their friends who were going through the process. I talked with some who were very successful in retirement and some who were dismal failures. The major differences between retirement success and failure always seemed to be forethought and planning.

My role model for retirement (and other things) was a guy named Tony. For a number of years, I worked for Tony. During that time he taught me a lot about my job but even more about life.

Tony was and is a guy who is always on the go. His favorite saying is "You can rest when you are dead, because you will be dead a long time."

By the time Tony retired at 62, he owned a house in France and a time-share in Cancun. He was on the board of directors of a couple of companies. He skied, windsurfed, played a decent round of golf and was in great health. Tony has now been retired for more than 20 years and is still as healthy and as busy as ever.

My worst retirement example is a guy I ran into in Florida who was retired early as the result of a large corporate merger. When I met him, he was in his early sixties. He had been retired for about five years and said that he hated retirement. I asked why and his response was "I don't play golf or softball, and I don't like card games. I exercise for an hour every morning and then watch the stock market every day on CNBC."

Ugh, what a life. Obviously, he hadn't figured out what he really wanted to do.

Although it may not be easy, as you approach retirement you must develop answers for those two key questions. Again the questions are:

"Who and what are important to me?"

"What do I really want to do with the rest of my life?"

If you don't have any passions, or at least interests, outside work, you had better begin developing them.

CHAPTER 4

THE SPOUSE

Opinions expressed by the man of this house do not necessarily represent the opinion of management.
— a sign in a Cracker Barrel restaurant

Since I am a man, in this book, I will use "spouse" and "wife" interchangeably; but some of the lessons I learned (often the hard way) apply to the working member of a married or similarly committed couple, whatever his or her gender. Although I realize there are other ways people arrange their lives these days, I only have experience in one model. I need to add a disclaimer that my expertise even in this area is not always sufficient to keep me out of trouble with my spouse.

For many years, my wife and I led very different lives. She was busy raising the kids, being a chauffeur and shopper, taking care of our home and planning our social activities. My work included a considerable amount of overnight out-of-town travel. During the week, I played some business golf occasionally, and in good weather I played golf with my friends on the weekends.

I still remember the first evening after our youngest went off to college. My wife set the dinner table but this time with only two place settings. She said, "Tonight we are going to talk with each other."

Except for vacations, which we took annually, we had not actually talked with each other for almost 20 years. We hadn't had to, because one or both kids were always there. As I remember, on that most memorable first evening at home alone, I suggested that we just watch television instead. This turned out to be a very bad move on my part. My penchant for saying things like this is why I disclaimed spousal expertise above.

Several nights of dinner discussions followed. As I began telling my wife that I wanted to retire, the discussions got more and more intense. One night my wife asked, "What will you do in retirement?"

I said that I wanted to travel and play golf.

She pointed out that I was already traveling and playing golf and that I was getting paid to do it. I responded that I wanted to go where I wanted to go, when I wanted to go, and to see what I wanted to see. I did not want to continue just to go from an airport to a hotel, to an office and back to an airport.

A couple of weeks later, THE KEY ISSUE erupted.

"I don't want you hanging around the house," my wife declared rather loudly. "I have a life, and I don't want you to ruin it."

I responded weakly that I only wanted to have a life also.

It took me some time to recognize that my wife had already retired – albeit gradually – over the preceding five or six years, without our feeling any need to discuss it. Thanks to modern appliances and financial circumstances that allowed for occasional household help, cleaning and cooking hadn't demanded a lot of her time. Her main job had been taking care of the kids. As they grew older and required less and less of her day-in, day-out attention, she had replaced those hours with recreational and community activities she shared with her friends. She'd built a retirement life for herself. Now it must have sounded to her like I planned to demolish that by waking up one Monday morning and asking, "What are we going to do today, honey?"

I assured my wife that that wasn't my agenda. I had plenty of things I wanted to do on my own. She wouldn't need to entertain me. But I have to admit that until Sue Ann raised the issue, I hadn't thought about how my retirement would impact her. I'd considered it *my* decision. Boy, was I wrong.

For anyone who is married or in another form of long-term, committed relationship, retirement is a joint decision. That's one of the main reasons to start planning for retirement, together, early. In fact, the honeymoon is a good occasion to begin the discussion; but even if you're approaching your thirtieth anniversary, it's important to have that talk, and to revisit it whenever some major change in your career or personal life occurs. This is true whether a couple has the kind of traditional arrangement Sue Ann and I have, whether both plan uninterrupted careers or whether one will stay home while the kids are young, then return to the workforce.

Retirement issues are a huge but not generally acknowledged source of marital discord. Sociologists don't seem to rank them up there with problems with finances or infidelity; yet even long and apparently healthy marriages end all too often when the spouses are in their sixties and seventies, with something vague like "irreconcilable differences in personality" given as the cause. I suspect that in many of these cases, the trigger is unresolved conflict around retirement.

Suppose both spouses work outside the home. They live in Chicago. One of them wants to retire at 58, after the youngest of their three kids graduates from college, and move to a warmer climate and travel the world. The other still gets a lot of satisfaction from the workplace. Their careers are out of sync. This can be a particular challenge for couples in which the wife suspended her career while the kids were young, then went back to it once they were in high school. Now, thirteen years later, the wife's career is finally taking off. She's got the title and the respect and the office with the window. The husband, on the other hand, is tired of the 45-minute commute, tired of the tedious staff meetings, tired of stuffing his roll-aboard into the overhead bin, tired of the cold, windy winters.

When retirement looms for either spouse, an out-of-sync, two-income couple has several tough choices to negotiate: The spouse who wants to retire can do so but delay the dreams of warm climate. Or that spouse can postpone retirement by a couple of years, and the other can accelerate it by a similar amount. Or they can embark, temporarily, on a long-distance marriage (almost always a more difficult challenge than it appears at first). They may need professional help to work these things through in a way that leaves neither spouse feeling resentful.

Once I recognized that *my* retirement would have to be *our* decision and my wife began to get a little more comfortable with my desire to retire, we started thinking about where we might want to spend our time, at least during the winter months. During those years, the company I worked for held lots of meetings in the scenic Scottsdale, Arizona area. Over the years, I came to love to visit Scottsdale, with its warm winter weather and its beautiful desert golf courses. About six years before I was planning to retire, I took my wife with me on one of those business trips. We spent the weekend in a golf community north of town that I particularly liked.

I have heard it said that people either love or hate the desert. On that particular weekend I learned how true that was the hard way. My wife hated the desert.

Several days after we returned home, I finally got the courage to ask her what she thought about my chosen retirement location. She made a few comments that set a new direction for our search.

First she said, "If I thought you were going to ask me to live in a concrete block house with a dirt backyard, I would have stayed in West Virginia."

Now, the villa that we rented for the weekend was a very nice home built of concrete block but covered tastefully with stucco, as most of the homes in that area are. She was correct about the backyard. The community required that all of the yards be "natural" to save water. That meant bare dirt decorated with large, medium and small rocks and a few plants that were largely thorns.

Then she asked, "Where is my favorite place in the world?"

"Hawaii," I quickly answered.

She responded, "Did that desert look anything like Hawaii?"

I had to be honest. "No," I said.

My wife completed this conversation by declaring, "We will be spending our retirement in Naples, Florida."

This was an excellent suggestion on her part. We had also visited Naples on business. It did look a lot more like Hawaii than Scottsdale did, and we had a number of friends and acquaintances who had retired to the area. In any case, my search was quickly redirected to southern Florida.

Retirement is a huge change for a spouse as well as for the retiree. As I learned, any time you spend on retirement planning without involving your spouse likely will be wasted. Make sure that you have your spouse firmly on board before you get started.

CHAPTER 5

FINANCIAL PREPARATION

Money is better than poverty, if only for financial reasons.

— *Woody Allen*

I began my retirement financial planning in my forties with a goal of being able to retire at age 60, and I did.

The most important retirement choices are dictated, or at least influenced, by your financial situation. There are many books that discuss retirement financial planning in detail. The time to read these is in your forties, but it's never too late to benefit from their authors' expertise.

Although I won't attempt to address in detail financial preparation for retirement and money management once you retire, I will give you the benefit of my experiences and what I learned, sometimes the hard way, as my wife and I made our important retirement choices. I was fortunate to be reasonably successful financially in my career. However, when it comes to preparing for an enjoyable retirement, maximizing your income isn't enough. You also need to be concerned about how much you spend, and therefore how much you are able to save. As my mentor Tony once told me, "The way to get rich is simple: Make a lot of money, and don't spend any of it."

If I'm an expert in anything, it's engineering, not financial planning; and I've always believed in calling on professional help when considering important decisions outside my area of expertise. I was fortunate to connect with financial planner John Krolikowski, owner of Trebuchet Consulting in Pittsburgh. John not only helped me get ready for retirement; he still helps me with a financial "check-up" from time to time, and he was kind enough to allow me to call on his expertise for this chapter.

I started by asking John when he recommended people start planning for their retirement. John surprised me by saying that he had just provided advice to a young lady 24 years old who was just starting her first job. He told her to begin by putting ten per cent of whatever she earned into her company's savings plan, even if the company only matched the first four or six per cent. He also recommended that each time she got a raise she add one per cent until she reached the plan's limit for contributions.

Obviously, the 24-year-old had no idea what type of retirement she might want. The idea was for her to start saving early, and regularly, for whatever she might want to do in 30 or 40 years.

John's point is that there are two things you can do with each dollar that you earn – after you pay taxes, of course. The first is to support your current lifestyle. Funds in excess of those costs can then be saved to meet your intermediate goals, such as educating children, and your longer term retirement goals.

Your lifestyle choice, both during and after your working life, may be the most important retirement decision you will make. As an example, John pointed out that earning a million dollars a year isn't enough if you spend $1.2 million a year. Saving for retirement isn't about how much you make; it is about how much you spend, and therefore how much of your monthly cash flow you can save and invest. Saving is the key, since the money you save is the money that will compound to provide for your future needs.

When discussing the importance of saving and of having those savings compound, John reminded me of the Rule of 72. When you divide 72 by an assumed investment return rate, you get the number of years that it takes to double your investment. For example, if you assume a six percent rate of return, it will take 12 years to double your investment. However, at an eight percent rate of return, your money will double in nine years. One lesson of the stock market and home equity crash of 2008 and 2009 is to be conservative when predicting your rate of return. As John likes to say, "You can save money over time but not overnight."

While I was working, Sue Ann and I lived relatively modestly. We lived in the same house for 25 years and paid off the mortgage early by adding extra equity toward our monthly mortgage payments.

I drove mainly purchased (sometimes used) Pontiacs, while some of my friends and colleagues were driving leased or purchased BMWs and Mercedeses. Sue Ann and I always paid our credit card bills in full each month.

The unspent cash flow we were able to save and the compounded earnings are now being used to fund our Florida lifestyle, my golf passion and our travel. I am glad that we chose the conservative route.

Most 401K and other employer-offered savings plans offer models that enrollees can use. John recommends using one or more of these to help with your goal-setting and financial planning. Most of these models allow you to make assumptions about what you will be able to save and invest and see what the outcomes can be or to work backwards from the amount you think you will need in retirement, and the date when you'd like to retire, and see how much you'll need to save each year. As with many topics these days, you can also get help with retirement financial planning online. For example, on http://www.walletpop.com/calculators/retirement there are several retirement models that can answer many questions as you prepare yourself.

One caution about 401K savings plans is that having a diversified portfolio is important. You may remember that many Enron employees had all of their savings allocated to their company's stock and lost it all when Enron went bankrupt. Rather than trying to pick individual stocks or funds for your retirement savings plan, you may want to consider one of the age-based or degree-of-risk-based options available.

During our brief discussion, John also offered the following bits of advice:

1   If you plan to purchase a retirement home, make the purchase before you actually retire. That way, if the house or condo costs more than you had planned, you can work an extra year or so to pay off the difference.

2   Before you retire, make sure you understand the income, sales, real estate and death taxes in the state where you plan to live.

3   Never change your investment choices based on short-term performance. Knee-jerk reactions based on the last quarter rarely add value over the long term.

4   If you have the ability to defer income into a company nonqualified plan, this can be a very attractive way to defer taxes, grow your investment on a pretax basis and help with post-retirement cash flow planning. Just be sure that your company is in good financial shape and will survive throughout the required multiyear payout period.

5   The importance of cash flow doesn't end when you retire. You still need to spend less than you bring in, in order to be prepared for unforeseen expenses that might occur.

6   Consider utilizing a financial planner to help you set your goals and to develop plans to meet your goals. Choose an independent professional, not one associated with a brokerage firm, and arrange payment on an hourly

rate. That will assure that your advisor has no financial interest in recommending one form or investment of another. Then, like an annual dental examination, schedule a once-a-year checkup to make sure that you're on track to meet your goals.

7   This one is for sure: PowerBall is not the answer!!!

John also recommends reading *Kiplinger's Personal Finance Adviser*. This monthly magazine will keep you focused on the future and give you good tips to help you on your saving-for-retirement journey.

It is never too early or too late to start your retirement financial planning. In fact, a few hours with a financial planner might be the best graduation or wedding gift you could give a young person you care about.

One of John's most important pieces of advice is number 5: The importance of cash flow doesn't end on the day you retire. If anything, attending to cash flow becomes even more important. Retirement is a wonderful time to enjoy the fruits of your work (or better yet, your inheritance, if you were lucky). That's the good news. The qualifier is that living in retirement and doing what you like to do does cost money, so you need to consider financial decisions carefully and plan conservatively.

While you are working, you are always making more money. There's always another paycheck. With the exception of recessions, you could expect to get a raise in pay every year. Sometimes, you may have gotten a promotion with more pay. Maybe you received stock options. And in good times, you might have received a bonus, too. The downturn that began in 2008 may have caused you to put off that last day at the office by a year or two or scale back your travel plans, but the basics remain the same: You will have to think differently about money once you retire.

When you retire, you suddenly realize that whatever money you have now is likely to be the most money that you will have for the rest of your life. For the first time, your expenditures may exceed the income you receive from investments and pensions. It's a little scary at first. It takes getting used to; at least it did for me.

There are costs and risks that you need to be concerned about in retirement. But if you are conservative and have done a good job of saving and financial planning, retirement can be wonderful time for enjoying life.

In retirement, the way you will spend your money will likely fall into seven major categories:

1.   Providing a place for you and your spouse to spend your Active Years and your Middle Years and covering your basic living expenses,

2.   Funding activities to keep you healthy, entertained and happy,

3.   Traveling,

4.   Helping with expenses for children, grandchildren or parents,

5.   Providing for your care during your Declining Years,

6.   Passing on to your children or other family members, and

7.   Donating to causes that you care about, or even leaving a public legacy.

While all seven have value, my wife and I have decided in the short term to focus on the first five.

Some folks in retirement like to say that their focus is on "spending their children's money." I have come to believe that this is a good way to think about spending discretionary financial resources, especially for Categories 2 and 3 above.

Of course, issues beyond your control can sidetrack your plans or even throw them off completely. The credit and stock market crisis that began in October 2008 dominated the news for several years. The economy was as bad as I have ever seen it.

After a few weeks of terrible economic headlines, my wife asked me, "With all that is going on in the markets are we were going to be okay financially?"

I responded, "As of now, it looks like we will be just fine, but the kids have taken one hell of a beating."

Not everyone is as financially fortunate as my wife and I have been. I had a well-paying job as a corporate executive. I received raises and promotions. Sue Ann did an excellent job of managing the household expenditures so that we had money to save. We were spared major crises with our children and our health. But even if you have more limited means, you can still lead a pleasant retirement. Provided you plan well, set a realistic budget and discipline yourself to stick with it, you can have a satisfying life. For example, if you will be living on Social Security and a teacher's pension, you can donate time, rather than money, to the causes you care about.

You and your spouse will have to set your own priorities for the seven categories above. It deserves open discussion, a lot of thought and a firm agreement.

CHAPTER 6

GETTING STARTED

A journey of a thousand miles begins with a
single step.
—*Lao Tzu, Chinese philosopher (c. 604 BC – 531 BC)*

Earlier in this book, I suggested that you start asking the following key retirement questions while you are in your forties: "Who and what are most important to me?" and

"What do I really want to do with the rest of my life?"

Note the use of "I" in the above questions. This is in conflict with the real world of retirement for married couples, since retirement is a *we* proposition. But even though planning for retirement for couples is definitely a two-person job, if you don't know what's important to *you*, as an individual, or what *you* want to do with the rest of your life, you can't discuss, let alone negotiate, retirement issues with your spouse. Of course, if you are single, you can do whatever *you* want.

If you are past your forties and have not yet answered the two questions above, don't stop reading, just get started exploring those two questions *now!*

The question "What do I want to do with the rest of my life?" must be answered before you make any other retirement decisions. It even influences the age at which you retire, because if what you want to do is climb the highest mountain in each state of the union, for example, you'd better plan on retiring early.

To explore that important question, it helps to break it down into pieces, biting off smaller choices, such as the following:

Do I want to watch my grandkids grow up? Every day?

Do I want to travel and see the world? Or the U.S.?

Do I want to be able to be outside year-round to play tennis, golf, fish, boat, swim, run, snow ski, hike, etc.?

Do I want to be near a major university for learning or a city with major performing arts and museums for culture?

Do I want to live near my current friends? Or my family?

Do I want to move closer to my kids? Or my parents?

Do I want to be with other retirees like me, or would I prefer to be around people of all ages?

Do I want to be in the same time zone as my family?

Do I want to be near a major airport and/or a major medical center?

Do I want to be near a professional sports team?

Do I want to be near a casino?

Do I want warm winters and hot summers? Or cool winters and mild summers? Or pretty much the same temperature year-round? Do I like high or low humidity? How much do I hate bugs?

Do I want to have one year-round home or seasonal residences?

I am sure there are many other choices. I know folks who made retirement decisions based on each of the above. These choices are difficult because most people value more than one of these options.

"What do I want to do with the rest of my life?" is likely the most important decision that you will make from here on out, because this decision drives everything else. This decision can also inject significant stress into a marriage. One of my friends wanted to be south in the winter so that he could play golf, but his wife wanted to stay north to be around the grandchildren. This is a common dilemma.

A relatively large number of people get this decision wrong the first time. Many move from their chosen first retirement location after only a couple of years, because they discover that what they thought was important to them (in terms of activities, amenities, even the time they wanted to spend with the people who were significant to them) wasn't and that other factors were. This route to self-knowledge is expensive, stressful and time-consuming.

Since my wife and I agreed that we wanted warm weather in the winter, we agreed to head for southwest Florida like many other so-called "snow-birds." Although we hope that we will have grand-children some day, we don't have them yet, so that was not an issue for us.

What you want to do with the rest of your life is the biggest factor in determining where you choose to live – and where you live will impact everything else. If you are half of a couple, start early to reach an agreement that will satisfy both of you. And if you are widowed, divorced or a lifelong single, I strongly recommend avoiding getting involved in a serious relationship until you know the answer to this question. Otherwise, you may find yourself embarked on a romance with a built-in, irreconcilable conflict.

CHAPTER 7

WHERE AND WHEN

Home is where the heart is ...and where it is warm.

— Dave

If you, and of course your spouse, decide that in retirement you either want to move permanently or seasonally, you have a lot of work to do and a lot to consider. But before we get to that, let's start with the "when" of such a move. Remember that your Active Years will last only a relatively short number of very valuable years. In the earlier example in Chapter 2, that precious period could be seven to twelve years, depending on whether you retire at 65 or at 60. Your Active Years only amount to about nine to 16 percent of your total life expectancy. But when you retire, your Active Years could be 40 to 50 percent (or even more) of your total remaining years. Believe me, those go by really fast!

So you do not want to waste any of your valuable Active Years in searching for a location, buying or building a home and furnishing (or worse, decorating) it so that you can start to enjoy your retirement.

You should get all of this done while you are still work-ing so that you can start enjoying retirement when you actually retire.

As you know from Chapter 4, my wife and I agreed on a general area (Naples, Florida) for our winter home based on trips we had taken while I was working. We also had a number of friends and acquaintances who had chosen the same area for vacations or retirement homes.

In 1999, five years before my planned retirement date, we began to develop a list of specifications for our "dream" retirement home. In our case, it was to be a free-standing house, in a golf community, on a golf course, with the front of the house facing south and a pond in the back between the house and the golf course. As you can see, we were very specific.

My wife also insisted that the house be smaller than our current home, but with the same number of rooms. In addition, she wanted none of the rooms to be smaller than the same rooms in our current home. (How she hoped to accomplish both goals escaped me.) As a final step, we agreed to a "firm" price that we absolutely would not exceed.

We sent these specs to a friend-of-a-friend real estate agent and scheduled a trip to Naples the week after Thanksgiving 1999. Our objective for the one-week trip was to purchase our dream home.

During that week, we saw about ten houses, any of which I could have lived in happily. However, thank goodness, my wife is much more discriminat-ing. While we did not buy a house on that trip, we did find a great lot and a wonderful builder who had built houses with a floor plan that we loved. We signed agreements, made a down payment and were off and running.

As I am sure you suspected, the original estimate for the cost of the house was about 20 percent above our absolute, not-to-be-exceeded, "firm" price. Not surprisingly, our builder could not figure out how to make the house smaller and still have the number of rooms and room-size constraints my wife required.

For the next two years, Sue Ann diligently oversaw the construction and decorating of our dream house. In May 2001 we took possession at a final cost of about 30 percent above our absolute, not-to-be-exceeded, "firm" price as a result of several change orders during construction.

During the winters of 2002, 2003 and 2004, my wife, along with our miniature dachshund Rudy, wintered in the house with yours truly visiting on weekends. During the winter months in these early years, my wife also entertained a lot of weekend guests who were looking to spend time in the warm Florida sun. (More on guests later.)

Unfortunately, this story did not end totally happily. Shortly after I retired and moved in, I was informed that while the house was just fine for my wife and Rudy, it was too open and noisy when I was around.

Here I made what initially appeared to be a huge mistake but turned out wonderfully. I told my wife that we could move if she could find a house that worked better for her, met all of our original specifications and was totally furnished to her satisfaction. I added the last criteria to attempt to control the decorating time and costs associated with a move.

Well, to my surprise, she did find a home that met all of our criteria. In August 2005, we moved into a slightly larger furnished house in a gated golf community, with the house facing south and a pond between the back of the house and the golf course. Of course, my dream of controlling the cost of decorating proved to be just that. The good news is that this change has turned out great for both of us.

While our first house was open and therefore could be a little noisy when I was watching TV or on a call in the study, the real problem was that my wife did not feel comfortable in the slightly older and well-established community. Although choosing the correct area of the country and the correct type and size of your housing unit are important, picking the correct community for both of you is even more important, as Sue Ann and I found out. (It's so important, in fact, that I've devoted an entire chapter to it, Chapter 10.)

To get started, first decide on the area or areas where you think you'd like to spend your retirement years. Take a few trips to the area and spend a little time looking and asking about the area. Next, settle on what kind of retirement home you want and can afford; but then, before you begin house-hunting, determine the kind of community where you and your spouse can feel at home and where you will enjoy building new social connections.

CHAPTER 8

LOCATION

There are only three important criteria in real
estate: location, location and location.
— every real estate agent I ever met

That old real estate saying about location applies even more so to retirement. The issue of where to retire – in terms of climate, proximity to relatives, scenery, available amenities and cost of living – presents a seemingly infinite number of choices. After you've decided when to retire, and maybe even before you've set a date, this will be the first decision you will need to make as you approach that major transition, and one of the most important.

The key to an enjoyable retirement is to find people who like to do what you like to do. This is true whether you decide to spend your retirement years in your current location or to spend part (or all) of the year someplace else. Finding like-interested people is most difficult if you decide to stay in your current community, especially during the winter months if you live up north. Many of your friends and the other people you know will still be working; or if they've retired, they may be spending the winter at another location.

Whatever your recreational passion, magazines that cater to it run ratings every few years on the best places for readers to purchase a vacation or retirement home. For example, *Links Magazine* publishes a *Golf Real Estate Guide*. The 2008-2009 issue listed 26 golf communities as "Best for Golf," 20 as "Best of the Best," 17 as "Best for Value" and seven as "Best for Golf and Boating." In all, 151 communities merited the magazine's notice. Publications aimed at retirees are another source of comparative information. Depending on the magazine, you might want to take some of these recommendations with a grain of salt, especially if you notice that every place listed has purchased a nice, splashy ad. But they offer a place to start.

I love to play golf. In the winter in Florida, there are lots of guys who also love to play the game and who can do so any day of the week. However, when my wife and I traveled back north for the summer, I had much more difficulty finding "playmates," primarily because most of my friends were still working. The weather was fine for golf, but my buddies were available only on weekends – when every golf foursome in town was competing for a tee time.

The best way to begin to make your location decision is with a map. Start with where you are living now. Then ask the following questions:

Will my current location be where I want to live year-round once I retire? Can I do what I want to do there all year?

Do I need to have a second location for all or part of the year so that I can pursue my favorite activities in retirement?

Do I want to be able to drive to my retirement location or will I have to fly? If I'll have to fly, what are the flights like between my current location and the locations I'm considering? How far away from the new location is a major airport?

Do I want a year-round retirement home, or will I keep my current home, at least for awhile?

Another important consideration for Sue Ann and me was whether the state we were considering for a retirement home had a state income tax. There are currently seven states that do not tax income: Alaska, Florida, Nevada, South Dakota, Texas, Washington and Wyoming. (This comes from Money-zine.com, November 2008, as does the information that follows.) There are two states that only collect taxes on dividend and interest income: New Hampshire and Tennessee. Vermont and California have the highest incremental state income tax rate – 9.5 percent and 9.3 percent respectively. Six states have only one income tax bracket, or what is called a flat rate, charging their residents one rate on all income: Colorado (4.63 percent), Illinois (3.0 percent), Indiana (3.4 percent), Massachusetts (4.35 percent), Michigan (3.9 percent), Pennsylvania (3.07 percent) and Utah (5.0 percent). Missouri has the largest number of tax brackets (ten) ranging from 1.5 percent to 6.0 percent. I suggest you check this site or others as you begin your specific planning.

The presence or absence of a state estate tax can also be a significant consideration, as can whether a state is a community property state, in which an entire estate passes, untaxed, to the spouse unless a will names additional heirs. None of us wants to confront our mortality; but if you find a place where you want to spend the rest of your life, you'll probably die there, and that will be where your estate is probated. These laws can change any time a state legislature meets, so it's important to check for the most current information.

For my wife and me, weather was a second key consideration, since our chosen activity (golf) requires warm weather. One place to start investigating potential retirement sites is by looking at average temperature and rainfall levels. Below are average January and July weather data for a few potential retirement locations shown here as examples (from cityrating.com/cityweather.asp, November 2008).

AVERAGE WEATHER FOR SPECIFIC LOCATIONS

	JANUARY			JULY			
	AVE TEMP	HUMID- ITY %	RAIN FALL in.	AVE TEMP	HUMID- ITY %	RAIN FALL in.	DAYS OVER 90
SAN DIEGO CA	57	58	1.8	71	67	0	0
LAS VEGAS NV	46	32	0.5	91	15	0.4	30
TUCSON AR	51	32	0.9	87	28	2.4	29
PHOENIX AR	54	32	0.7	94	20	0.8	31
SAN ANTONIO TX	50	60	1.7	85	54	2.2	29
ASHVILLE NC	36	59	3.3	73	62	4.5	5

CHARLESTON SC	32	63	2.9	75	60	5	8
SAVANNAH GA	49	55	3.6	82	57	6.4	22
JACKSONVILLE FL	53	58	3.3	82	59	5.6	24
TAMPA FL	60	60	2.0	82	63	6.6	21
FT MYERS FL	64	57	1.8	83	60	8.3	25

NOTE: "Humidity" refers to average afternoon humidity, rainfall is in inches, and the last column reflects the number of annual days where the temperature tops 90 degrees Fahrenheit. The temperatures shown in the table above are 24-hour averages (day and night). The afternoon high temperatures will be much higher than the numbers shown in the table.

As you can see, there are significant differences from one location to another. San Diego has the smallest January to July temperature difference, with a change of only 14 degrees. On the other hand, Las Vegas has a change of 45 degrees.

A word here for those considering retiring on a modest budget: Housing prices and cost of living in general vary widely from location to location within the Sunbelt. For example, daytime highs in January and July are almost identical in Tucson, Arizona, and San Antonio, Texas, and the number of days with temperatures above 90 degrees is the same. Yet, as I write this, you can still find a two-bedroom, two-bath townhouse in San Antonio for under $100,000. It won't be on a golf course, but a well-tended municipal course will be nearby. And if you're a veteran, you can save money by shopping at the base exchange (BX).

When choosing a location, one final item to check is bug and other critter levels. I was recently at an outdoor party at a coastal community in South Carolina where the sand fleas or "no-see-ums" were particularly aggressive. The person greeting the group mentioned that he was thankful for the sand fleas because "if we didn't have our sand fleas, everyone in Ohio would want to live here." I quickly decided that I was one of them who didn't.

Before you settle on any location, visit it at different times of the year. You need to experience for yourself the temperatures, humidity and bugs. Do not trust the natives or the current residents. Everyone will try to convince you that their choice was and is the best choice, even if it's not – or wouldn't be for you or your spouse.

Other considerations that should be checked out are the level of medical care readily available, access to cultural and arts events in the area, access to sporting events and the number of good places to eat. My list also included the quality of the golf courses, while my wife's list included the quality and accessibility of shopping.

We chose Naples, Florida, primarily for its lack of a state income tax, for the good air service to the Midwest and the East Coast from the Fort Meyers airport about 30 minutes away, and for the warm and relatively dry winter months.

Summer weather in Naples is a different matter, but I have gotten used to it.

Since your retirement location choice should involve careful thought, research and visits to potential locations, you should start this investigation several years before your potential retirement date. Visiting locations on your retirement short list can make for an enjoyable series of vacations, in addition to helping you make your decision. (One tip: Rather than booking a hotel, rent a house or a condo, to give you a sense of the practical side of life, such as convenience and quality of supermarkets.)

Do not get yourself into a position where you have to waste any of your Active Years in retirement working on where you are going to live instead of actually enjoying your hard-earned retirement.

CHAPTER 9

A HOUSE, A CONDO, A HOME

Home is where your friends are.

— Dave

If you have decided that you'll need a second residence, or that you'll want to relocate, in retirement, you'll have several very important interrelated decisions to make. Among the many options which need to be carefully considered, the place to start is "How much can you afford (or do you want) to spend?"

This may seem straightforward, but let me assure you that it is not. A financial advisor once told me that most people who get into financial trouble in retirement do so by overspending on a house. This happens because they underestimate the total expense of owning a house, including the considerable ongoing costs. To start with, there is the cost of buying the house plus some usually minor fees and taxes.

Next comes the cost of furnishing the house. When I asked my wife in 2001 what she thought it might cost to furnish our house, she replied, "How should I know? I haven't even started looking yet." No opportunity for a budget here. So for cash-flow planning, I made what I thought was a reasonable estimate and doubled it. Not even close. I guess I should have spent more time watching "The Price Is Right."

One way to avoid the uncertainty of the cost of furnishing and the considerable amount of time wasted looking at furniture and "dustables" is to purchase a furnished house or unit. This is certainly easier and quicker; and if you're relocating, full-time or seasonally, to another part of the country, the décor may fit the climate and lifestyle better than what you had back home. The downside of this approach, in my experience, is that the survival rate for furniture and "dustables" purchased in this manner is 70 percent or less. "There is nothing wrong with it. It is just not me!!!" is something I have heard too often. (By the way, "dustables" are all the things that sit out on your tables and chests, serve no useful purpose and must be dusted regularly.)

We bought our second retirement house fully furnished. Before we purchased it, Sue Ann assured me that she loved (or liked or at least could live with) all the furniture and that only a few throw pillows would have to be replaced. A few weeks later I returned from golf to find two trucks in the drive. One was taking furniture from the house to a consignment shop. The second was unloading the replacements. And this was not just a few pillows. Even today after living in our second Florida home for five and a half years, another room is currently under refurbishment.

Furnishing a house or condo can cost a bunch, but it is primarily a one-time expense. The costs that get people into trouble are those that are ongoing. Many of these are driven directly by the original amount paid for the house. These items include real estate taxes, insurance, electricity, gas, heating oil, maintaining air conditioning and heating units, condo fees and assessments, and association fees. In general, the larger the home, the larger these costs.

But that is not the entire list of expenses by any means. There are other costs that are not necessarily driven by the price or the size of the house but nonetheless can add up to significant monthly expenditures. These include such things as telephone, water, cable or satellite TV, internet connection, lawn and shrub care and pool cleaning. And then there are the break-down repair costs that inevitably occur. We have repaired and replaced more appliances than I care to remember.

While a retirement place is expensive, it is probably what you have worked so hard for so long to be able to buy. Just be careful to consider all the expenses plus the cost of doing what you really want to do, such as travel, golf or boating.

If you only want to relocate for a few months of the year, you might consider renting. This is also a good way to learn about an area before you make a major commitment. And if you and your spouse want to spend your Active Years exploring different parts of the world, you won't be tied down. You can spend January through March in the Bahamas one year and in Costa Rica the next. And you can let someone else worry about replacing the roof when it needs it.

Once you are comfortable with the cost question, the second question is "What type of residence do I want?" Again, there are many choices from recreational vehicles (drive where you want), to condos (high rise, mid rise or low rise), to villas or zero-lot-line units, to freestanding houses (small, medium, large and even huge). As you begin to work on this issue, you should start by addressing the following questions:

Do I want a place for short stays (rent?) or a place where I plan to spend several months each year or even move to permanently now or later?

Do I expect family or friends to visit often and/or use the place when I'm not there?

Am I willing to rent out the unit in the early years or even part-time in all years?

Do I want a smaller or a larger place than I'm used to?

Do I want a yard? If so, would it be maintained by me or by a homeowners' association?

Especially if I plan to travel a lot, how about a high-rise or a smaller condo?

Do I want to buy a residence that is new or used? Or do I want to build?

Do I want to buy the house or unit furnished or unfurnished?

Many people choose to start small in a new location with a condo or a villa of some sort, especially while they are still working. The advantages are packaged maintenance, known costs, the ease of coming and going and generally a low hassle factor. This approach also lets you try out a location with a relatively smaller investment or even by renting. Many folks are happy to enjoy this way of living long-term, but others find condo living too confining for longer stays; and once they are sure where they want to be, they move into larger quarters.

A word of caution is needed here on condos. Check out the payment record of all members and the financial condition of the developer before you buy one. During the recent financial crisis, unfortunately many folks living in condos found out that even if they could pay their condo fees, some of the other owners could not pay. In this situation, the condo members who could pay had to pay more to cover the deficit caused by others. This can be particularly painful if there are only a small number of residences in the condo association. The situation can be even worse if it is a new building or development and the developer gets into financial difficulties.

In our case, we are dog people, so a high-rise condo was out of the question. My wife wanted to be on the beach; but where we live, given our budget, that meant a high rise. As I mentioned earlier, my wife wanted to go smaller with strict restrictions, so we started with a detached house that was about the same size as the one we had lived in for 25 years.

In retirement you have a lot of time to do things. Some people spend their time moving (or at least they did until the housing market collapsed). I know of people who started in a condo, moved to a house, moved to a villa, moved to a house and now live in a condo. In my view, they should have spent more time playing golf or fishing. In addition, this approach doesn't work when the housing market is flat, making it much easier to purchase a place than to sell it.

What type of unit to live in is the second most important retirement decision. Over-spending or making other bad decisions can have devastating financial consequences. Be very careful with this choice!

CHAPTER 10

A GREAT COMMUNITY

Goldilocks said the porridge in the first bowl
was too hot. In the second bowl she found that
the porridge was too cold. But after tasting the
porridge in the third she said that it was just right.
... paraphrased from "Goldilocks and the Three
Bears" by the Brothers Grimm

Communities are like the porridge that Goldilocks tasted. Finding the "just right" community is very important. So what are the criteria to consider? There are three keys to identifying the "just right" community for you: activities available, age of the residents and maturity of the community.

Activities are the easiest. If you like to boat, look for communities with docks or launching ramps. If you like to golf, look at golfing communities. The only way to get this choice wrong is if you have not decided what you really want to do or even like to do or if you and your spouse cannot agree on what you want to do. (You want to ski, and she wants to play golf year-round.)

Age of residents is also fairly easy. To determine whether a community is age-compatible, first decide whether you want to be in one where most residents are retired or nearing retirement or one that includes people of all ages. Remember, choosing the latter may mean tolerating shouts of "Marco! Polo!" by 12-year-olds doing cannonballs while you're trying to swim laps. And if you choose a community where everyone is 55 or older, will your grandchildren be welcome when they visit?

Once you (and your spouse) choose one style of community or the other, you will need to spend some time at the ones that interest you. Take a couple of hours in the common areas, such as the country club, exercise facility, swimming pool, and tennis courts. Talk to folks. Get a feeling about what they like about the community, where they are from, what they like to do inside the community and how old they are. If you are comfortable with all the conversations you have, and if the average age appears to be less than five years older than you, that community is probably okay at least from an age-of-residents standpoint. If the average age is seven or more years older than you, you probably should move on.

Your new community is where you'll make your new friends. If you're 60 and the average age is 68, that's not too bad initially. But, as you look ahead ten years, you'll be 70, while your neighbors will be nearing 80. You'll still be in your Active Years, but who will you enjoy them with?

The issue of maturity of the community is trickier and can be more important.

A "mature" community is one that has been in place for ten to 15 years or longer. It will likely be fairly well built-out and full of folks who have been there for many years. Friendships and social groups will probably be well-established, and it may be hard for a new, "younger" couple to fit into the social structure.

A "maturing" community is one that has been in place for five to seven years. It would probably be 50 to 80 percent built out. The average person would likely have lived there for two to three years. This community would have experienced significant influxes of new, "younger" residents each year of its existence and would probably be much more receptive to new entrants.

An "immature" community is one that is less than three years old. It would probably be less than 40 to 50 percent built out. The good news is that in "immature" communities everyone is new, relatively young and looking for friends. The downsides are that years of building (with its dust, debris and noise) lie ahead, and this is the riskiest time for the community's developers. A developer with financial problems usually means a community with financial problems.

Communities age just like their residents age. My parents moved into a "maturing" golf community on the east coast of Florida in 1982 when they were in their early sixties. Twenty-eight years later, they still live in that same community, as do some of their remaining friends. As you can imagine, their community is beyond "mature." Both the community and its golf club have had a very difficult time attracting younger retirees for many years.

The above is an over-simplification. But in our particular case, we built our original retirement dream house in a "mature" community. The people were nice, but we never felt like we fit in. It was hard to find a golf group. We were invited to a few neighborhood parties but not the big private community-wide parties. Everyone was older in general, and they seemed comfortably established in their social groups. While this was a little difficult for me, it was a really big deal for Sue Ann.

Our second community was a "maturing" community. My wife was greeted and made to feel welcome by neighbors and many others. I was invited into golf groups. Initially, we felt very comfortable and still do six years later. For us, at our second community, the activities, ages and level of community maturity were all "just right," and it has been wonderful.

Making sure that you will fit in and be welcomed is the key to finding the "just right" community. Don't take the word of the salesperson or the representatives of the developer. Do your own homework!

SECTION TWO

THE FIRST DAYS OF THE REST OF YOUR LIFE

Successful management of change requires
that you actually change something.
— *Dave*

CHAPTER 11

RETIREMENT, DAY ONE

My wife said, "Whatcha doin' today?"
I said, "Nothing."
She said, "You did that yesterday."
I said, "I wasn't finished."
— from the Internet

If you ask someone who is about to retire, "What do you plan to do on your first day of retirement?" their response is likely to be "Sleep in." This may be a reasonable response, but it isn't a good way to get started with the rest of your life.

Retirement is a huge change. Most people will have worked 30 or 40 years in a very structured, fast-paced environment. These retirees now face 20 or more years (hopefully) with no forced structure and no set timetables.

The most important task for a new retiree is to create a new structure. In retirement, your days do not need to start as early as they may have when you were working. You can actually sleep in, assuming that you can get your mind and body to adjust after years and years of getting up at a given time. (Because I couldn't adjust, I still get up at 7:00 a.m. every morning.)

I believe that the best way to begin retirement is to start out by doing something very different. The old routine has to be broken. Some folks take a long trip or a cruise. Others begin an extended stay at a second residence or a few weeks at a rented condo or beach house. There needs to be a distinct break between your old life and your new life.

A week in your old life consisted of five work days and two play or rest days. Your new life can consists of seven play days or seven rest days and/or combinations thereof. In retirement, every night is Saturday night. You can go to a movie any evening, or better yet, any afternoon. In fact, after a brief period of time, you will actually have trouble remembering what day of the week it is.

I now keep track of the days of the week by counting the number of newspapers we get. If we get two (local plus *USA Today*), I know it's a weekday. If we get only one small one, it's Saturday. And Sunday is the big paper day. You may snicker as you read this, but just you wait and see.

My structure includes eating breakfast out every day (see Chapter Twelve on "The Spouse in Retirement"), followed by playing golf (see Section Three: "Golf: My Key to a Successful Retirement"), which is followed by lunch with the guys.

Whatever your structure, try to do something on a regular basis. You can always change it later, but when you enter into retirement, begin by doing something regularly.

Retirement has its own resultant stresses that must be dealt with. My advice is to plan your retirement structure so that you NEVER have to ask your wife either of the two following questions:

"What are we doing today, dear?"

or

"What's for lunch, darling?"

Adding the terms of endearment on the end of these questions will not improve the way that they are received or lower the level of stress that they will bring into your life. You need to make a life of your own, doing what YOU like to do.

Because life as a retiree is so different, you must be well prepared before you start retirement. You need to do a lot of preparation to get ready for Retirement Day One! If you are about to retire and are not well prepared, reread Section One of this book and get to work.

CHAPTER 12

THE SPOUSE IN RETIREMENT

My wife doesn't mind if I hang around the house.
She only gets mad if I try to come inside.
— a retiree who wishes to remain anonymous

While retiring from work and entering an unstruc-
tured world is a big step for you, if you're a guy, your
entering your wife's domain can be an even bigger
adjustment for her. As the result of your retirement, she
now gets a lot more of you and most likely a reduced,
fixed income to boot. What a deal! For a woman
who's worked outside the home all or most of her married life, this doesn't seem to be as much of an issue.
She probably knows what she wants to do on Day
One of her retirement. She's got her activities planned,
for the day, for the week, maybe even for the year ...
because, even though she's been working fulltime,
she's also likely to have been the one in charge of
making the family's plans all along. If the two of you
retire at the same time, she's probably going to act in
much the same way as she always has.

A husband's retirement will be much more traumatic for a woman if it involves a permanent or even a seasonal move to a new location. In this case, she gets a lot more of you, she gets the reduced, fixed income, and she has to give up her friends and routine and start her life over with only you. Talk about tough!

My wife struggled mightily with these upcoming changes in her life as I got closer and closer to retirement. One day when I got home from work she said, "I figured it out. I just need to get into the bucket."

It seems that on that day there was an interview of Ellen DeGeneres in our local newspaper. Ellen told a story about her move into a new house. Her old house had an in-ground fish pond. She enjoyed watching the fish in the pond so much that she had a similar pond built at her new house.

When it came time for her to move, she tried to catch the fish in a bucket to relocate them to their new home. This proved to be very difficult. The fish had no way of knowing that the new pond was bigger and better than their current pond. They only knew that they were secure and happy where they were.

Ellen pointed out that people are many times like her fish. We are comfortable with where we are and what we do. Many times we are unwilling to try different things or to take chances, because change is scary. But sometimes we just need to "get into the bucket" and move on.

My wife did "get into the bucket" and is very glad she did.

Retirement is not an easy change for couples, because both husband and wife need to get comfortable with their new lives. They need to make new friends, both together and separately, and new rules need to be developed.

As a gag gift, I used to give refrigerator magnets to the wives of retiring friends. The magnets read:

I am not your secretary,

I am not your mother,

You will have to do it yourself.

Several recipients of these magnets said that after awhile when their husbands asked them to do something, they only had to point to the refrigerator as the poor guy's head dropped. Obviously, my retiring male friends were not all that thrilled with my gift.

In our case, the new rules were never formalized or actually even discussed. Nonetheless, we both came to understand them. Following are the ones that I now follow after having been critiqued and criticized over the past six years:

1. The newspapers are hers first. I can look at them only after she is finished.

2. Breakfast is only served at home if I make it for myself or if I wait until she gets up and is ready to eat.

3. Lunch at home is out of the question.

4.   My study door is to be kept shut when I am using the speaker phone or watching CNBC or sports or a movie, etc.

5.   If I ever attempt to help organize my wife's activities or her parts of the house (which is everything but my study and the garage), I am reminded that if I need to boss people around I should get a job.

My relationship with my wife has gone very well in retirement since I learned these unwritten rules. She is busy with her friends playing golf and mah jong and shopping. I am enjoying my friends at my "adult day care center," also known as the golf club. (See Chapter 21.)

As a couple we love to go to the movies with friends or by ourselves and to eat out with friends or alone and occasionally even to play golf together. (See Chapter 26.) And, of course, we take trips together, as you will see in Section Four.

As a side note on eating out, where we live it is important to be known by the owners or at least the managers at a couple of good restaurants. The restaurants do not have to be expensive. (I think restaurants are better if they are not fancy or pricey.) This is important because we live in a very seasonal area. During peak season you can wait a long time to get a table in any restaurant. But if you are a "regular," or better yet a year-round customer, a small additional tip will always get you to or at least near the front of the line.

You can only have a happy and successful retirement IF your wife is also happy with her new situation. ***Do not minimize the importance of her happiness.*** Work hard to stay out of her space and help her through this huge change in her life.

CHAPTER 13

JOB ONE: STAYING ALIVE

Whether you're a brother or whether you're a mother,
you're stayin' alive, stayin' alive.
Feel the city breakin' and everybody shakin',
and we're stayin' alive, stayin' alive.
Ah, ha, ha, ha, stayin' alive, stayin' alive.
Ah, ha, ha, ha, stayin' alive....
the Bee Gees

For a number of years, Ford Motor Company publicly advertised, "Quality is Job One." That seemed pretty strange to me since it was obvious that the Japanese car manufacturers had been taking over the U.S. automobile market with higher quality and more efficient cars for years. The quality of Japanese cars apparently had been missed by those to whom it was most important: the American automotive industry.

Maintaining your health in retirement is truly your "Job One." To fully participate in your precious Active Years, you must be mobile and healthy.

My retirement plans included playing a lot of golf and traveling to see the world, both of which require the use of my legs. Remember that my doctor had recommended a local hospital's four-week, two-hour-per-week, diabetes management program, which I attended. I learned that my diabetes was controllable through diet and exercise. This became the roadmap for my Job One, and six years later I am still working on it.

Doctors' appointments, flu shots and check-ups are also an important part of my retirement program. After all, once you retire you will have the time; and thanks to Medicare, after age 65, medical care is damn near free.

Things do and will happen to you as you age. Catching issues early is often the key to staying healthy or quickly getting back to good health.

We all know that lifestyle choices can make a big difference in our health, mobility and longevity. Overeating, excessive drinking and smoking are things I see a lot of among retirees in my area. We have been warned for years about the risks of these chosen behaviors. As you enter retirement, you need to think seriously about the implications of these lifestyle choices on the rest of your life.

A good friend of mine, who was an avid smoker for most of his life, had planned to quit once he retired. Unfortunately, one year into retirement, at age 58, he was diagnosed with Stage Four lung cancer. He was dead in four months.

I once heard a quote that caught my attention and stuck with me: "I plan to live forever, and so far so good." A little unreasonable perhaps, but making and following a plan to extend your life and mobility for as long as possible is a worthwhile effort. In fact it should be your Job One.

I have another friend who was very successful at a variety of things. He believes that you can do anything you want by following this simple formula:

Decide what you want.

Make a plan to get it.

Follow the plan.

This is a great formula that you can use for planning your Job One. If you have not already ordered *Younger Next Year* by Chris Crowley and Henry S. Lodge, M.D., do it now. Working out, walking, golfing, playing tennis or biking, combined with eating correctly, not smoking and refraining from drinking excessively can certainly help you extend your Active Years.

In addition to physical health, retirement requires that you also take care of your mental health. Your mind, like your body, seems to work better the more that it is used. Watching television does not seem to provide much exercise for the mind.

Now that you have time, you can and should read the books that you always wanted to read. I decided to read all the books written by James

A Michener. These are wonderful to read, especially before you travel to a different part of the world. You should not visit Hawaii or Alaska without reading Michener's *Hawaii* or *Alaska*. They provide terrific introductions to the history and geography of those places, wrapped entertainingly in compelling stories. His other books are equally interesting.

After a couple of trips to Spain, and after reading Michener's *Iberia*, I read Ernest Hemingway's famous novels set in that country, *For Whom the Bell Tolls* and *Death in the Afternoon*, and *A Farewell to Arms*, set in Italy. I like to blend these classics with current bestsellers.

To make reading or at least getting a good book, easier, I asked for and received a Kindle for Christmas. I have enjoyed reading using this amazing little device. If you like to read, get one.

I also suggest that you continue to read newspapers and magazines, in print or online, to keep up with international, national and local news and issues. I particularly enjoy the daily challenge of the Sudoku puzzles in our local paper and *USA Today*.

The Internet is a wonderful way to communicate with friends, satisfy your curiosity or simply waste time. Spend an hour or two on your computer each day. While researching the travel section of this book, I stumbled onto Wikipedia, the web encyclopedia containing facts on just about anything that you might find interesting. It's easy to access what it has to offer. You just search by topic using Google or whatever other web browser you prefer.

In retirement you have lots of time to do whatever you want. Make a plan, and commit to dedicating some of that time to maintaining or improving your health and mobility and to keeping your mind sharp and well exercised.

Make your plan, and follow it!

CHAPTER 14

MANAGING YOUR CALENDAR

You can rest when you are dead,
because you will be dead a very long time.
— Tony Dorfmueller

I hope you remember my mentor at work and in life, Tony, whom I introduced in Chapter 3. Tony's wisdom included the quote above. This quote has kept me focused on always staying busy and active.

Another important skill that Tony taught me was the correct way to utilize a very important tool in retirement, a calendar.

To start, Tony suggested that I get a calendar with a box for each day of a month. I have always used a spiral bound 8 1/2 X 11 inch calendar with a month shown on two pages, side to side when opened.

Tony's next instruction was to put something in every square. This may sound simple, but filling in all the boxes requires lots of decision-making and planning ahead.

The sequence I recommend for filling the squares consists of the following:

First enter what you need to do and when.
Second, enter what you want to do and when.
Finally, think about how you will fill in the rest of the squares.

My annual calendaring works like this:

1. First, I put the few regular meetings that I need to attend each year in the proper squares.

2. Second, I add the two major trips that my wife and I take each year. (See Section Four: Travel.)

3. Then, I work with my traveling golf groups to set dates for our two or three annual guys' golf trips. (See Section Three: Golf: My Key To Successful Retirement.)

4. Next, I add the dates of social events such as our local Broadway series dates and our club social and golf events.

5. Finally, I schedule my regular medical check-ups. For me, this consists of two appointments each with my internist, dentist, dermatologist and eye doctor.

The above fills about 100 of the 365 squares on my calendar even before the year starts. Many of these 100 days require planning and early commitments. Loading up next year's calendar with the above items should be a high priority at the end of each year. It might help to make it one of your rituals for the week between Christmas and New Year's.

Time goes by very quickly in retirement; and, remember, time is limited, and it is precious. People who live day to day or even week to week will miss a lot of opportunities that they can only enjoy during their relatively few Active Years.

Take the time to plan ahead and schedule ahead to make your true desires a priority and to maximize your precious Active Years.

CHAPTER 15

GUESTS AND VISITORS

Fish and visitors stink after three days.
— Benjamin Franklin and my mother

Retirement begins as a transition between your old life and your new life. If you decide to spend retirement permanently or even seasonally in a new location, old friends and associates will make the transition to your new life both easier and more difficult. This is an area that you need to understand fully prior to your actual retirement.

Before you start casually inviting family, friends, associates and even acquaintances to visit your new retirement home, read this section carefully. Then, have your wife read it, and have a frank discussion about the positives and negatives of guests.

Old friends are an important and comfortable tie to your past life. But old friends can also be a deterrent to your moving on into your new life.

Initially, inviting old friends to visit you makes the transition to retirement easier. Visits maintain your ties to the past, and you get a chance to show off your new residence and your new location. The downside is that guests require time and attention. You will want to show then around and entertain them, and they will certainly expect no less.

Invariably, sooner or later, this will cause you to miss an opportunity to attend an event that would have allowed you to meet new people in your new location. These conflicts will prevent or at least delay your assimilation into your new life.

If you spend all or part of each year in a new location, your new residence can become an alternative (and free) seasonal vacation spot for your old friends and associates and even some casual but aggressive acquaintances. After all, among the reasons you chose his spot for your retirement were its pleasant climate and its abundant recreational opportunities – which also make it an attractive vacation destination. This is especially true for potential visitors who are stuck for the winter in a much colder region.

Friends of mine had a relatively casual acquaintance call and ask if he and his family could spend two weeks visiting my friends at their Florida home. My friend, a good soul, finally agreed to a four-day stay but was amazed by the request and did not enjoy the visit.

Once Sue Ann and I began staying seasonally, during the winter, in southwest Florida, we were surprised at how many friends and acquaintances from the cold north were willing to come stay with us. Being friendly folks, we had casually invited everyone we knew to "come visit us in Florida." Many of them took us up on our offer.

The first winter my wife and our miniature dachshund Rudy spent in Florida, I commuted down from work on eleven weekends. For ten of those, we had weekend guests. I thought this was great, primarily because I was a visitor myself.

My wife, on the other hand, felt like she was running a bed and breakfast. Buy the food, clean the house and wash and change the towels and sheets: that was her schedule every week. There was little time for her to meet new people, to get involved with neighbors or other members of the community or even just to relax.

One other trap that you can fall into is the "annual visit." Before you know it, friends or acquaintances will begin to lay claim to a certain week on your calendar. For example the second week in February can become the week for the annual vacation visit of your friends X and Y.

When you have assimilated into your "new life" routine, it is hard to take a few days off (or worse a whole week off) to entertain guests. I know that this sounds selfish, but at some point your new life and new friends will become a higher priority than your old friends (and a much higher priority than your old acquaintances).

Once we finally decided that the number of visitors had to be reduced, we initiated the following strategy. When a friend or acquaintance called to say he or she would be down the second week in February as usual, we began to respond, "We're looking forward to seeing you, too. Let us know where you'll be staying, and we'll plan to get together for dinner."

This was usually followed by silence on the other end of the line and then, "We'll let you know." Strangely enough, many of these trips have never materialized.

I am not suggesting that you should have no guests. Best friends, family and in my case golf member-guest partners are always (or almost always) welcome. Remember, if you are actively filling your retirement days with what *you* really want to do, you won't have a lot of time for entertaining guests.

And even when your house guests are family members or close friends, remember my mother's advice: Two or three days is plenty long enough.

CHAPTER 16

GET INVOLVED WITH PEOPLE

No one is in charge of your happiness but you.
— anonymous

In retirement you have a lot of time to fill. This is either good news or bad news, depending on how you approach it. To solve the problem of filling lots of time, all you need to do is to decide what you really love to do and find other folks who love to do the same thing.

This is somewhat more difficult if you are married. (I guess this also applies to lots of things.) Your wife also needs to find friends who like to do what she likes to do. And then you both need to find couples who like to do what both of you like to do.

The place to start is first to find the "just right" community for you, as described in Chapter 10. Sue Ann and I have found that finding new friends and making acquaintances that have like interests is fairly easy, provided you choose the correct community. In retirement, almost everyone is looking for new friends and for things to do with others.

Although you probably won't enjoy the company of everyone in your new community, my observation is that you can expect to find a group of people whose company you will enjoy.

In our "maturing" community, we found making friends to be very easy. There are lots of activities for men, women and couples. With a little initial effort, you, too, will discover that you can be busy socially morning, noon and night, if you choose.

Even in the "right" community, there will always be a few people who seem bent on making life uncomfortable for everyone else. These people are commonly known as "jerks."

One of my favorite cartoons of all time was a "Far Side" cartoon by Gary Larson. It showed God at a chemistry bench. Behind him was a shelf with glass jars filled with ginger-bread-like people. The canisters on the shelves were labeled Blacks, Browns, Caucasians and Asians. In front of God was a glass globe into which he had placed people from each of the jars. In one hand, he held one final canister labeled "Jerks." As God reached his other hand into that last canister full of "Jerks," he said: "This should make life interesting for everyone else."

So when I come into contact with a real jerk, I smile and remember that this is just God's way of making life interesting for the rest of us. Taking this approach makes dealing with these inevitable indi-viduals much easier for me.

Retirement is much more enjoyable if you find people you really enjoy being with. It isn't hard. Everyone else is looking also. But it does take getting out and meeting people. It's certainly worth the effort.

CHAPTER 17

STAY FLEXIBLE FINANCIALLY

*It's when the tide goes out that you find out
who has been swimming naked.*
— *Warren Buffett*

In 2008, the tide went out.

The Standard & Poor's 500 index dropped 39% for the year and was off a full 50% in November. The Dow Jones Industrial Average finished the year down 34%, up from a low of off 44% in November. The NASDAQ ended the year off 41%.

To make matters worse, those markets didn't hit bottom until early March 2009, and they kept bouncing along after that.

Most of these losses occurred in the eleven months between May 1, 2008 and March 31, 2009. These were terrifying times for investors, workers and retirees. Many people saw their life savings reduced sharply. Workers looked at their dropping balances in their 401K retirement plans and begin to call them their 201 K accounts.

To make matters worse, a New York investment manager named Bernie Madoff turned himself in for running a Ponzi scheme that apparently lost $65 billion of his investors' money. His scam totally wiped out the savings of many workers and retirees.

As the media explained at the time, a Ponzi scheme is a confidence game in which the con artist, who may previously have been a legitimate investment manager, uses money from new investors to pay out unusually high returns to longer-term investors. These attractive returns continue to attract new investor money and all goes well until the new money stops coming in. Then the game is up. As the publicity that followed in the wake of Madoff's crash reminded all of us, if a deal seems too good to be true, it probably isn't true.

The only good news during these very difficult months was that retirees who were receiving Social Security from our government got a 5.8% benefit increase for 2009.

As a side note, since I retired and began to receive Social Security payments at age 62, I never forget to thank my working friends who are contributing to my retirement. In fact, I have offered to give them a picture of me to put on their desks along with those of their families, so that they will remember all of those that they are working so hard to support. No one has taken me up on this offer yet.

I will only mention in passing that the U.S. government's Social Security program has many of the attributes of a Ponzi scheme, since the early "investors," like me, are now being paid by the current contributions of the later "investors" who are still working today. I wonder how long this scheme can last.

The market drop of the late months of 2008 and the first quarter of 2009 would have been unthinkable to most of us only six or nine months earlier. This plunge was precipitated by the sub-prime mortgage mess, which was based on the assumption that house prices will always go up. And for about 50 years or so, housing prices did just that.

The largest investment that most folks hold is the value of their house. We were taught over the years to borrow as much as possible and buy the biggest, most expensive house that we could get.

We were also taught that over time the stock market would go up at about 7% per year, apparently forever. Here again, leverage was available and encouraged. Some people bought stock on margin. Others also received options on their companies' stock as part of their employee benefits package.

As a result of those terrible ten months, retirement savings were significantly reduced, house prices dropped precipitously, and many workers lost their jobs. As of mid-2010, the economy still looks very weak. A few of my retired friends have had to go back to work, others have sold assets such as second houses or boats at distressed prices, and many others have had to drop out of country clubs and curb such pleasures as travel.

Unfortunately, market crashes aren't the only financial difficulties that a retiree can encounter. There are at least four other types of problems that can lead to financial concerns.

The most obvious problem, if your parents are still living, is their care. With people living longer these days, many times they outlast their savings and their ability to live on their own. Long-term care insurance can cover much of this, which is why a sound financial plan should include policies for parents and parents-in-law, as well as for the couple approaching retirement. Parental care can be expensive and can go on for a long time.

The second potential problem area is your children. They will probably (in my case hopefully) give you grandchildren. This can turn your children's two-paycheck household into a one-paycheck household with higher expenses. Or your children or their spouses, or maybe even both, may get laid off. What kind of help would you be expected to provide in any of these situations?

Your health or your spouse's or even your children's could require a substantial outlay of funds if serious health issues develop or if you or they lose their health insurance. Once you and your wife reach 65, most of these expenses will be covered by Medicare, although you should shop carefully for Medicare supplement plans that pay for costs not otherwise covered. If you retire before age 65, as I did, you might have some large exposure if you develop problems before you reach eligibility age.

A fourth circumstance, one more common than I had suspected, is divorce in retirement. Before I retired, my wife and I led full and active but very different lives, as I discussed in Chapter 12. Retirement has brought us a lot more time together. We've been able to adjust, but not all couples do so successfully. Little problems that were ignored for many years can blossom early in retirement. These little problems can become big problems, big enough to break up a marriage that has endured decades. If either of you senses this happening, seek professional help early, from a counselor, a therapist or your religious leader. Divorce can be expensive (not to mention very painful and disruptive) for both parties and for the rest of your family.

This chapter is not meant to scare you out of retirement. It is intended to encourage you to be conservative as you make your key retirement financial decisions and as you invest your retirement savings. The best advice, as always, is if an opportunity appears to be too good to be true, it isn't.

Also consider what I have been told by some investors. Apart from your home (or homes), you should never own any assets that cannot be sold by 4:00 p.m. on any weekday. Illiquid assets are really difficult to unload in tough times when you may need the money the most.

When it comes to financial forecasts, John Kenneth Galbraith may have put it best when he said, "We have two classes of forecasters: Those who don't know – and those who don't know they don't know."

Expect the best, but plan for the worst. There is a lot that can go wrong.

CHAPTER 18

HOW DID WE GET SO OLD?

How old would you be if you didn't know how old you was?

— *Satchel Paige*

The biggest surprise for me in retirement has been how fast the days, months and years go by. The second biggest surprise has been how little I can accomplish even though I have all the time in the world.

About six months after he retired, my boss of many years called me one day just to check in. I was very busy at work but was delighted, as I always had been, to get some more direction or advice. But instead of offering direction or advice, he asked, "Do you know what I have done today?" After I responded, "No," he said, "I got up at 8:00, read the local newspaper and the *Wall Street Journal*, went to the golf course and hit some practice golf balls, came home and made lunch. I am about to sit down with my book and probably will take a nap." He continued, "It is amazing how little you can actually accomplish if you put your mind to it."

Retirement operates in a lower gear. The days still have 24 hours and the weeks seven days, but it seems to take much more time actually to accomplish anything. This is even truer for my parents who at 93 and 88 never seem to have time to read the instruction book on how to operate the new cell phone that I got them for Christmas.

My wife and I stay busy, at least by our new standards. I play golf every day and do projects after I get home. She plays golf and does other stuff; I am not sure exactly what she does, and I am not about to ask.

It seems impossible that we have been retired for over six years. But worse, I have just celebrated my sixty-sixth birthday. People say that age is just a number. My number is getting pretty big. I don't feel any different today than I did ten years ago, and I am probably in better shape now because of my level of physical activity.

I think Ronald Reagan was correct about age (and many other things). After he turned 39, Reagan stopped celebrating birthdays and began celebrating anniversaries of his thirty-ninth. On that basis, I have just celebrated the twenty-seventh anniversary of my thirty-ninth. Now I feel better.

An analogy that I like is "Life is like a roll of toilet paper. The closer you get to the end, the faster the roll turns."

Another quote I heard recently is that inside every old person looking into a mirror is a young person wondering, "What the hell happened to me?"

Life certainly zips by when you are retired. You think you have lots of time to do things. Not true! Stay busy and plan your Active Years to do the things you have always wanted to do before you get too old or immobile to do or enjoy them!

CHAPTER 19

LIVE THE DREAM!

*Your attitude towards life defines not only who you
are, but the quality of life you are after.*
— *from the Internet*

I am not sure who originated the quote above.
It came to me over the Internet along with several
other positive life messages. I like this quote because
I have always tried to be a positive and optimistic
person. I also like spending time with fun and optimistic people.

Sometimes I think that optimistic people, or
perhaps happy people, are simply those with low
expectations. Having low expectations means that
you are much less likely to be disappointed by the
many trivial things that we encounter every day.

This is exactly the opposite of what I was taught
while I was working. In fact, one of my employees
once asked me, "Will you ever be fully satisfied no
matter how well we perform?" My answer at that

time was, "No, because I know we can always do better."

Today, I have much lower expectations about food quality and service when eating out, of my friends, and especially my wife, to be on time and not to forget promises made, of my children and their issues, and especially of my golf game. As a result, I almost never have a bad meal or a bad experience or, more importantly, a bad day.

On the other hand, I know people who never have a good experience or a good meal. They are always complaining about this or that or everything. It seems to me that they think that everyone is out to make them miserable. As a result, they tend to make everyone around them miserable, also.

It is all about the two types of people who answer the old question "Is the glass half full or half empty?" differently.

No matter how you answered this question when you were in the high-pressure world of your work, I suggest you consider the "glass is half full" point of view for retirement and lower your expectations. This will improve your life and the lives of those around you.

Remember, in retirement you can do what you want, when you want, with whomever you choose. (Of course, that assumes that you can get your wife to agree.) And, on average, you will have 17 to 22 years to enjoy your retirement. So, why waste your time and energy complaining? Certainly no one else wants to hear it.

For me, retirement is truly "living the dream." I love it! I love playing golf, spending time with my wife, partying with our friends and traveling. (I will address golf and travel in the last two sections of this book.)

Put on your happy face, be positive and optimistic, If you do, I'll bet that you will enjoy retirement as much as I do. Be Happy!

SECTION THREE

GOLF: MY KEY TO A SUCCESSFUL RETIREMENT

---

*For me, if they had not invented golf, they could
not have invented retirement.*

— Dave

CHAPTER 20

"BUT WHAT IF I DON'T LIKE GOLF?"

Twenty-four hours a day, everybody has to be doing something.

— *Dave*

Maybe I overstated things when I suggested in the introduction to this section that retirement would be impossible without golf; but sometimes I really do feel that way. The one thing that all retirees have is plenty of time, and the trick is to fill as much of that time as you can doing things that you truly enjoy. As I survey my neighbors and friends, I find fishermen, wood-workers, tennis players, cyclists, swimmers and people who seem to live at the gym. Some of my neighbors spend five hours a day researching and tinkering with their investments, working on their family genealogies or playing on the Internet, especially on Facebook. Others spend an equivalent amount of time playing bridge, gin or mah jong (a current craze among the women in my community). Some retirees love to shop. Still others volunteer their skills to the causes they care about.

Although I'm not an expert on the joys and challenges of most of the above retirement activities, I do have some observations about one popular pursuit: boating. I just don't get boaters. Whether power or sail, boaters seem to have a couple of things in common. First, they are always lamenting the fact that the boat doesn't get as much use as they had hoped. Either the weather isn't right, or they can't find someone to accompany them, or getting the boat ready to take out has become just too much hassle. Or worse, they're unhappy that their boat is smaller than they really need for offshore sailing or for deep-sea fishing or for having a few other couples onboard for a cocktail cruise.

The most common complaint among boaters is the expense. Some wise wag likened sailing to standing in a cold shower tearing up hundred-dollar bills. Apparently, that's true of power boating as well. In addition to the cost of a slip at the marina or the gas gobbled during fishing trips, something's always breaking; water takes its toll on the hull, engine and mechanical equipment, not to mention the electronics.

We all know that buying a boat is easy – say, 1 on a scale of 1 to 10. But selling a boat is at least a 15 on that same scale. Nothing depreciates like a boat. Just visit a marina anywhere these days.

Here in Florida, all along the coast there are places that rent boats of many sizes; many come with a captain to do all the work. This strikes me as a wonderful solution to both the use and the ownership problems: If you want to take up boating in retirement, or if you've always been a boater, consider renting one when you want to and letting someone else worry about the ongoing, and the unexpected, expenses.

While I was still working, I was involved in several very worthy nonprofit organizations. However, when I retired and relocated to a new area, I chose to spend my time in different ways. But a good, long-standing friend of mine named Pete devotes a considerable amount of his time volunteering, and he enjoys it. So I asked him to share what he'd learned in the process. Below are Pete's words:

When I retired, I was assessing what I wanted to do to stay active and mentally occupied. A phone call from a business associate and friend helped get me organized.

The friend offered the following guidance: When planning for life in retirement, find five things in which to become engaged. You can select them from a variety of areas – a new business, sports, hobbies, volunteering, and learning – whatever appeals to you personally.

"Just find five things!" he said.

"Why five?" I asked.

"Because at any moment at least one could fall apart; so with five things to focus on, you'll always have something worthwhile to do every day."

[By the way, this advice was given to my friend by the same wise man named Tony who also gave me a couple of good tips that I related earlier in this book.]

As I developed my list of five, one of which was playing golf a couple of times each week, I included volunteerism. During my working career, I had volunteered on boards for our local homeowners' association, a home for challenged children and several trade associations. When I moved to our new home in Sarasota, I learned that as a retirement haven, the city had many retirees who were looking to volunteer for the local charity boards. So I took stock of my interests, and my skills, and with the help of a neighbor, I got involved instead with the local affiliate of a national nonprofit, Habitat for Humanity.

I had always had a personal desire to help provide shelter, food, or education to those needing assistance. My engineering background, desire to work outdoors, and enjoyment in building things led me to Habitat. After sorting out the Sarasota chapter's building process, I settled in on the framing construction team. After the slab is poured, our team builds the exterior and interior walls, does the roofing (including shingles), and installs all windows and doors.

At Habitat, we work side by side with the families who will be moving into the houses we build. Witnessing their joy and pride in their new homes is extremely satisfying to all the volunteers. The camaraderie of the work team adds to the enjoyment of building these homes.

As an added bonus, several members of my team and I have traveled to different cities to participate in Habitat construction projects in areas hit by natural disasters. One year we went to Gulfport,

Mississippi, to help families affected by Hurricane Katrina. Our second trip was to Cedar Rapids, Iowa, which had been devastated by floods.

I have benefited significantly from this experience by developing new skills and new friendships not only within the Sarasota chapter, but also in the distant Habitat affiliates where we have spent time.

Volunteering has met many of my needs. I have made new friends and have a purpose that gets me up and going several days a week, and I know that I am giving back to the community. I was fortunate to have had a successful career and to be blessed with a wonderful wife and family, and now I can give back to those in need.

I do believe the recommendation to find five things that you may want to do is great advice. And, while you're at it, give some serious consideration to making one of the five rediscovering golf or trying it for the first time.

CHAPTER 21

WHAT'S SO GREAT ABOUT GOLF?

*Golf is essentially a battle with self. And a solitary
one, too, across unforgiving countryside where
character and skill are both challenged to the limit.
Yet curiously, this inner conflict provides a wealth of
profound insights and perceptions from campaign-
ers who have pondered on their way of life and
why they play the game.*
— Michael McDonnell

I love golf. I've loved it since I the first time I teed off as a 10-year-old with my grandfather. Although I wouldn't go so far as to say that I live for the game, playing it with others is one of my greatest pleasures. Having more time for golf, during my active, mobile years, was a, if not THE, main motivation for my retiring early.

While I was working, I played golf with my buddies on most weekends, weather permitting; and late in my working life, I took an annual golf trip with a group of guys. (See Chapter 27.) In my business life, my colleagues and I also played a few rounds from time to time with customers or suppliers.

Now that I'm retired, I play golf every day that I can. Here on the west coast of Florida, that means seven days a week year round. I now tell people that I play golf for a living. But I always add: For me it is not much of a living but it is a great life!!!!

Playing golf every day provides some exercise, competition, lots of socializing with other guys and, not unimportantly, time away from my wife's domain.

My schedule involves leaving home each morning at 7:30; eating breakfast at the golf club with the guys at 8:00 while debating club, local, U.S. and world problems; warming up by hitting practice balls and practicing putting; playing 18 holes in competition with two to ten other guys; and eating lunch at the 19th Hole while we pay off our bets and repeat our discussions of the issues of the day. After all this, I still get home at about 2:30 every afternoon, which gives me plenty of time to work on my honey-do project list.

Because golf is about competing with yourself as well as with others, you can find out more about a person in a four-hour round of golf than you could in months otherwise. You can learn about his level of ego, his capacity to deal with frustration, his competitiveness and, most importantly, his honesty.

Most people think that golf is all about getting a ball from a teeing area into a hole; but I've come to recognize that, for us amateurs, golf is actually about three things: self-control, confidence and honesty.

For most people, self-control is the most difficult of the three. As someone once said, "Golf is a game where a round ball is moved to a hole by equipment ill-suited for the purpose." Because of this challenge, a typical round for most golfers, almost all of whom think that they are far more skilled than they actually are, will invariable include a lot of poor shots. And each of those bad shots can result in whining or cursing on the milder end or shouting, banging clubs on the ground, or even throwing clubs on the more aggressive extreme. It takes an incredible amount of self-control to complete a round of golf without exhibiting any of these behaviors.

Confidence runs a close second in difficulty. When preparing for a golf shot, it's very difficult to keep negative thoughts and self-doubt at bay. Will you hit it fat, or in the water on the right, or into the trap on the left? The worst shots for me are the three-foot putts with a little break to the right. Practice can help build your confidence, but it's always hard to trust your swing or your putting stroke when a couple of dollars are on the line.

The golf challenge that should be the easiest to manage seems to be very tough for many people. That is the issue of honesty. During a round of golf, the temptation to be less than honest comes into play in many ways, from moving the ball from a difficult lie, to placing the ball closer to the hole when marking it on the green, to choosing a more advantageous location to drop a ball after it is hit into a hazard, to misreporting the score at the end of the hole, to entering an incorrect score into the club's handicap system at the end of the round.

Most golfers have seen, and many have committed, all of the above infractions. They may seem like small things, especially in the context of a friendly game, but they say a lot about the character of a person.

The infraction that is of most concern to other golfers is the practice of entering incorrect scores into the club's handicap system. We all know about the "sandbaggers" who never put their best scores into the system. These are the folks who win all the handicap tournaments. These guys make great partners and very difficult opponents. Eventually, this practice will hurt the sandbagger, because it will result in comments from fellow club members and hard feelings.

The opposite of the sandbagger is the ego handicapper. An ego handicap is a handicap well below the player's true skill level. Because these players can't deliver the scores that their handicaps would indicate, these guys are great to play against, but they make terrible partners. It may take a psychologist to figure out why these golfers need to pretend that they're better than they are, especially in a game where handicaps are designed to level the playing field. But, whatever the reason, ego-handicappers would rather have a low handicap than win matches or tournaments. In some cases, these guys will enter incorrect scores into the club system. A more common practice for ego handicappers is to pick up their ball when their partner finishes the hole, assuming that they will always make the remaining, sometimes long, putt.

Golf is a great game, some have even said that it is the "greatest game," but it is only a game. In addition to trying to play to the best of my ability on any given day, and to enjoying the socializing, I try to focus on self-control and confidence. The honesty piece has always been relatively easy for me. I always finish the hole and turn in my correct score, no matter how good or how bad it might be. Using this approach, I think I win a little more than I lose. And I always have a lot of fun!

For me, golf provides exercise, competition, socialization, challenge and fun. I could not imagine retirement without it.

CHAPTER 22

PUT ANOTHER WAY: MY FAVORITE GOLF QUOTATIONS

Golf is 20 percent mechanics and technique.
The other 80 percent is philosophy, humor, tragedy,
romance, melodrama, companionship, camaraderie,
cussedness and conversation.

— *Grantland Rice*

Lots of golfers have tried to capture the essentials of the game in words. Some have hit verbal holes-in-one. Take the quotations below, most of which came to me recently over the Internet.

1. Eighteen holes of match play will teach you more about your foe than 18 years of dealing with him across a desk. –Grantland Rice

2. Golf appeals to the idiot in us and the child. Just how childlike golf players become is proven by their frequent inability to count past five. –John Updike

3. It is almost impossible to remember how tragic a place the world is when one is playing golf. –Robert Lynd

4. If profanity had any influence on the flight of the ball, the game of golf would be played far better than it is. –Horace G. Hutchinson

5. They say golf is like life, but don't believe them. Golf is more complicated than that. –Gardner Dickinson

6. If a lot of people gripped a knife and fork as poorly as they do a golf club, they'd starve to death. –Sam Snead

7. Golf is a day spent in a round of strenuous idleness. –William Wordsworth

8. If you drink, don't drive. Don't even putt. –Dean Martin

9. If you are going to throw a club, it is important to throw it ahead of you, down the fairway, so you don't have to waste energy going back to pick it up. –Tommy Bolt

10. Man blames fate for all other accidents but feels personally responsible when he makes a hole-in-one. –Bishop Sheen

11. I don't say my golf game is bad; but if I grew tomatoes, they'd come up sliced. –Arnold Palmer

12. A really good swing lasts about three rounds. –Jimmy Cannon

13.   You always meet a better class of person when you hit your ball into the fairway. –Bob Hope

14.   Golf is like marriage: If you take yourself too seriously, it won't work, and both are expensive. –Anonymous

15.   An interesting thing about golf is that no matter how badly you play; it is always possible to get worse. –Anonymous

Occasionally, my partners and I come up with some good ones.

1.   Nice drive! I don't go that far on vacation. – Jim H.

2.   Don't argue about what is fair! "Fair" is only about the weather. –Dave

3.   No matter how good or bad your round starts, don't get too excited or too depressed, because your game will always find you (and you will shoot your normal score). –Dave

4.   I have a problem. I just realized that playing golf seven days each week is not enough to improve my game. –Jim H.

5.   Having hooked the first drive of the season into the woods, Jim B. said "I will be glad when this #%*&ing season is over!"

6.   It is said that trees are 90 per cent air, but so are screened doors. –Marc H.

CHAPTER 23

JOINING A GOLF CLUB

We are programmed to receive. You can check
out any time you like, but you can never leave.
— Don Felder, Don Henley and Glenn Frey, "Hotel
California"

Choosing a golf club to join is as important a decision as deciding where to live. In fact, for most retiring golfers, the decision will be the same, since the community they choose will include their golf course.

You may be wondering why I selected the above lines from the hit by the Eagles for the quote introducing this topic. The reason is simple: I wanted to convey a cautionary message. Like the Hotel California, many golf clubs are "programmed to receive" but extremely difficult to leave.

Like communities, golf clubs have life stages. Although it's much easier to find a game at a new club than at a mature one, joining a new club may entail more financial risk. In fact, these days becoming a member at almost any club involves financial risk. Although the country is officially in economic recovery, the downturn that began in 2008 has caused tough economic times for even the most established golf clubs. Golf club annual dues are among the first extras that businesses trim and households cut when they experience a drop in income.

For anyone, but especially for a retiree, a club membership is an investment – an investment in a beloved game and in other social and recreational opportunities, but an investment all the same. That's why, now more than ever, it's important to take the decision seriously, to become informed about the different kinds of clubs, and to ask plenty of questions about the ones you're considering. In other words, do your homework!

In most parts of the country, there are three types of private clubs: membership fee clubs, bundled golf (or golf-included) clubs and equity clubs. Membership fee clubs require an initiation fee, which is usually not refundable. Bundled clubs are the focus of real estate developments built around golf courses where the initiation fee is included in the price of the house or condo you purchase. With bundled clubs, annual dues and fees are an ongoing requirement of the ownership of the house or condo. Equity clubs provide a member with an equity stake that may be redeemed in the future when the member leaves the club.

Both bundled and equity clubs present potential issues if you eventually want to drop out. For bundled golf clubs, you can only drop your membership and the dues and fees by selling the property. As long as you own your house or condo, you're responsible for those dues and fees.

Equity club memberships are a way for a developer to raise money to get a new club up and running, and these clubs function a little like a Ponzi scheme, except that everyone knows (or should know) what's going on before they join. The way these clubs work is that a new member provides cash in exchange for a certificate of equity, which may be recovered in the future when the member chooses to leave the club. The early equity members who leave are paid back through the funds collected from those who join later. Sound familiar?

The equity to be returned might be expressed as a percentage of what you contribute (e.g., 90 per cent of the initial amount), a percentage of the future equity sale price (e.g., 90 per cent of the equity price for new members when you leave) or as whatever price you might be able to get for your membership in a private sale, less a transfer fee. The problems with equity club membership plans lie in the details and in the future. There are a number of "fine print" issues that you need to understand before you decide to join an equity club.

1.   It is likely that you won't be able to cash out until the membership is fully subscribed.

2.   Once the membership is full, members who want to cash out will probably be accommodated in the order that they entered their names on a resignation list indicating their desire to withdraw from membership.

3. Once a club's membership roster is full, it will usually require that at least one new membership be purchased for each membership redeemed. It isn't unusual for a club to specify that two or more new memberships must be bought before an existing member can be cashed out. There may be an exception that allows a member to transfer the membership to the purchaser of his home if the golf club is part of a residential community.

4. A member who wants to withdraw from an equity club will almost always be responsible for paying the dues and fees until his membership is redeemed. Hence, the above reference to the song "Hotel California": "You can check out any time you like, but you can never leave" – at least, not until a perspective new member comes forward, cash in hand.

5. The most important clause is one that will likely say something like: "The Board of the Club may change the rules as they see fit to support the best interests of the Club."

6. Finally, you can expect to find another clause, stating that you should rely entirely on the membership documents and by-laws. Combined with Number 5 above, this means, in plain English, "You cannot rely on what we tell you we intend to do, because we have the right to change the club's policies whenever we think we need to."

It may sound like I'm totally against equity clubs, but let me assure you that I'm not. I currently belong to two equity clubs and have been a member of other equity clubs over the years. I have enjoyed being a member of these clubs; and up to this point, I have always been able to redeem my equity successfully when I've left.

Unfortunately, the experiences of some of my friends and acquaintances have been less positive especially after the financial crisis of 2008. You need to approach membership in any golf club, especially an equity club, with your eyes wide open and your brain fully engaged. I have seen too many people receive unhappy shocks when their equity club faced difficult times. To avoid unrealistic expectations, you may want to refrain from listing your club equity on your financial balance sheet.

Being a member of a golf or country club is a great thing in retirement. It is a source of social activities and wonderful friendships. Joining the correct club is an important social and financial decision and one you need to consider carefully.

CHAPTER 24

THE JOY OF NEW CLUBS

*The grass always looks greener on the other side
of the fence.*

— Unknown

Of course, golf also involves another kind of club, the kind you swing. Have you ever noticed that new golf clubs always work better than your old clubs? At least, they always work better for a week or so.

If you're a true golfer, you probably have five or six, or even ten, old drivers tucked away in the basement or the garage. And for sure, you have even more putters. Yet, when your game deteriorates, the first response is always to buy a new club, particularly a new driver or putter.

Before we get into why new clubs always work at first, let's start with why old clubs stop working or why a golfer's game goes bad. A friend of mine believes that a golf swing is like one of those combination locks that contain those small wheels numbered 1 through 9. When you're swinging well, it's like having each of the nine wheels set on its correct number, so that the lock opens. It's wonderful! The ball goes far and straight every time.

But just when you think you have your swing grooved, somehow the combination changes and the lock won't open any more. Worse yet, you now have to start turning each of the eight wheels again to find the new combination.

New clubs always "work" because they help you identify those new combination numbers. A new club looks different and feels different. Because it's unfamiliar, it will force you to focus on the basics of your swing or your putting stroke. With a new club in your hands, you'll be more likely to check your alignment, to focus on your posture and tempo, and to stand still and keep your head down. It's like taking a lesson. When the pro shows up, you tend to concentrate on doing things correctly; and even without his giving you any instruction, you begin to hit better shots.

I've found that changing clubs always improves my game. However, the good news is that you don't need to invest in new clubs; you can recycle your old drivers and putters just as long as they seem different. Of course, once these become familiar again, you'll revert to your old bad habits, and their benefit will be lost. But the same thing will happen with a brand new set of clubs. If you play regularly, my experience is that the "honeymoon period" with a new or recycled driver or putter is only four or five rounds.

Some of my friends point out that similar substitution of new for the familiar will also result in temporary improvements in other parts of your life, such as a house or a car. This is called "the grass always looks greener" effect.

But just because the grass *appears to be* greener, that doesn't mean that it *is* greener. Think any major change through carefully. As with the golf clubs, the answer might be to simply refocus on the basics with what you already have. It will be much cheaper in the long run.

CHAPTER 25

THE UNWRITTEN RULES OF GOLF

I know that I can play better than this,
but I never have.
— *Spiro Agnew*

Golf is a game of many rules. Those articulated in the booklet published by the United States Golf Association cover almost any situation that you can imagine. (You should always have a copy in the side pocket of your golf bag.) But they don't address the key areas that make a friendly round of golf enjoyable for the average golfer. For this reason, I've augmented the USGA rules with some helpful suggestions that the group I play with has developed over time.

1. In match play, it's okay to give strokes and putts, but not both on the same hole.

2. No one wants to hear why you missed your last shot.

3. No one wants to hear what you were trying to do when you hit your last good shot.

4.   Whining or mild bitching is acceptable if done tastefully and if the shot doesn't end up too much better than you thought it would.

5.   One of the things that will bother most players is noise or movement while someone is hitting a shot. All players should be very sensitive to this issue.

6.   Don't take putts when given if they are more than two feet from the hole. If you do, you'll tend to lower your handicap and lower your income. Putt them in if you can, but count them if you miss them.

7.   Don't re-putt every putt you miss. This holds up the game.

8.   Don't play for a meaningful amount of money. Big wins and big loses can be very harmful to friendships, especially if sandbaggers or ego-handicappers are involved.

9.   Never stand behind a player on the tees. On the green don't stand behind a player putting, and don't stand on the line on the other side of the hole.

10.   It's bad taste to fall down laughing if a player hits a shot into a hazard or worse.

11.   Never offer advice to your partner unless he asks for it. It's permissible to offer advice to your competitors, whether it's requested or not.

12. The Fuller rule states that "if you are out of the hole because of a bad shot, you are expected to stay out of the hole." This is one rule that I do enjoy breaking.

13. It is good golf courtesy to acknowledge good shots by the other players in your group. It is marginally acceptable to add the comment "I only wish I could be happier for you" if the shot was hit by a competitor.

If you and your golf buddies follow the above unwritten rules, in addition to the official USGA rules, you should be set to have a friendly, smoothly functioning group to play with. In the event that issues come up from time to time, trot out the famous quote from that noted Los Angeles philosopher Rodney King: "Why can't we all just get along?"

CHAPTER 26

COUPLES GOLF

Every now and then, we all need to be humbled.

— Dave

"Why are you wearing that shirt?"

"Are those the best shorts you have?"

"That hat looks terrible. Don't you have one that matches your shirt?"

"Why did you stop the cart here? The girls park over there."

"Don't drive over the hills!"

"Slow down!"

Yes, gentlemen, it's couples golf day. I actually like couples golf every now and then. It's a good break from golf with the guys, and it keeps me humble.

I have to admit that I don't spend a lot of time picking my outfits for golf with the guys. Maybe if I did, they'd appreciate my style. Nah! No way. You know they'd just make fun of me.

A day of couples golf reminds me how far short I fall of the sartorial ideal presented by those buff male models in the Brooks Brothers catalog, heading for the golf course with their maize yellow slacks perfectly coordinated with their Palm Beach green cotton sweaters.

Couples golf has also taught me the downside of offering advice, even when it's asked for. Maybe you've had an experience like this:

She says, "What club should I hit from here?"

I respond, "I would say a 6 iron."

She says, "I don't like my 6 iron. I'll hit my 5 iron."

"Okay," I respond.

She hits the ball fat, and it rolls short of the green. Then she says, "I knew a 6 iron wasn't enough."

It's hard to win an argument in this environment, but in my case, my wife does get a lot of strokes.

As we start out, she makes nine, six and four (par). Of course, the par with two shots is an eagle. Next is eight, seven, three (par). This par with two shots is a "1." Our round continues with some good holes and a few disasters.

What do you know! We win the tournament and receive a $28 gift certificate from the pro shop plus dinner for our $55 entry fee. I can't wait for the next couples golf day at our club. I'm already planning what to wear and working on keeping my advice to myself.

CHAPTER 27

TRAVELING WITH YOUR GOLF GROUP

There is nothing better than a golf trip.
— *Dave*

If you love, or even enjoy, golf, nothing beats a golf trip with the guys. Even better is a series of golf trips with the same group of guys over a period of many years.

My experience with road-trips-with-clubs started one afternoon after a round of golf when one of my buddies said, "I'd like to play golf in Scotland sometime." Another guy in the group responded, "Why don't we get a group together and go next summer?" Then the member of our group who typically takes on the role of leader and planner spoke up and offered, "I'd be happy to schedule the trip." And we were off and running.

Our leader did plan that first trip for our group of eight. It was 1998, and he chose one of those golf vacation services that provided a van and driver, scheduled all the tee times and booked all of our hotel reservations.

We had a terrific time in Scotland. We played 11 courses in eight days, ate good food, drank good beer and wine and had great conversations about every topic under the sun. We went in August, so the weather wasn't bad, except for one cold and very rainy day at the Carnoustie Golf Links.

In Scotland, we held our first competition. At our final dinner, we awarded our first Champion a framed photo of the famous 18th hole on the Old Course at St. Andrews. That same evening, we voted for our favorite course of the trip (Western Gailes Golf Club) and decided to get together for another golf vacation the following year. This time, our destination would be Ireland. Luckily, our leader again agreed to make all the arrangements.

In the summer of 1999, Ireland was blessed with reasonable weather. This time, we played ten courses in seven days, some in the Republic of Ireland (the south), others in Northern Ireland. Once again, we used a golf vacation planner to provide a van and driver and make all the local arrangements.

Because Ireland is much larger than Scotland, we had some long hours in the van as we moved from hotel to hotel and golf course to golf course, but the experience was worth every minute on the road. From the spectacular Olde Head Golf Links at Kinsale in the south to the wonderful Royal County Down Links (our favorite) in the north, it was a terrific trip. Again, we had one day of rain – and it was a lot of rain – appropriately at the Waterville Golf Links. But we completed the round despite the weather. When you travel that far to play, you play.

The following summer found us in the south of Spain on the Costa del Sol – also known as the Costa del Golf. This time, we were able to base ourselves at one hotel on the beach at Marbella and travel every day to visit one of the fine golf courses in the area. We played ten courses in seven days, enjoying great weather for our entire visit. And after golf, we spent the rest of the afternoon relaxing on the clothing-optional beach.

The courses we played in Spain were all very good. Some had spectacular views overlooking the Mediterranean Sea and one even had a view of the Rock of Gibraltar and of Morocco across the way. Valderrama Golf Club (our favorite) and Sotogrande were the best. I'm proud to say that to check the spelling of "Valderrama," I was able to refer to my Champion's framed photo of the famous 17th hole at Valderrama that hangs proudly in my office.

In Spain we rented two Renault vans and drove ourselves. One van was fueled by gasoline; the other was powered by diesel. One thing we learned on that trip is that if you fill a diesel-powered vehicle with gasoline, you'd better hope that you're next to the appropriate automobile dealership.

In 2001, at my suggestion, our group ventured to Cabo San Lucas, Mexico. Our scheduled travel date was September 25. Our leader had objected that it would be hot in Baja that time of year and that September was the height of hurricane season. I'd countered that the coast with its ocean breezes wasn't so hot and that it had been a long time since Cabo had been hit by a hurricane. Then, of course, the September 11 terrorist attacks happened. Even though we were all stunned and saddened, we packed up and headed south.

For the first five days, the temperature topped 100 every afternoon, with not much breeze. Then Hurricane Juliette hit. We had two days of hurricane-force wind and heavy rain. The entire area lost power, roads and bridges were washed out, and the airport was closed for a week. Unfortunately, all the golf courses were closed also. Luckily, we were staying in time-share condos east of Cabo and east of the major highway bridge that was washed away by the storm. Fortunately, we were on the same side of the peninsula as the airport. Although the building where we slept was without electricity for the rest of our stay, the main hotel in the complex had a generator, so we had plenty of food and drink, and a TV to watch, while we waited for the airport to reopen.

If this sounds like a vacation disaster, you don't understand guy trips. The hurricane just left more time for card-playing, discussing the world's problems and enjoying each others' company. Despite the enhanced fellowship, however, the group did vote unanimously to remove me from the planning committee for life.

That year also marked the end of our group's international travel, at least to this point. For the following nine years, our annual itinerary, and our favorite courses for each trip, looked like this:

2002	Michigan/Wisconsin	Arcadia Bluffs
2003	Naples, Florida	Calusa Pines
2004	Florida East Coast	Hammock Dunes (The Creek Course)
2005	Northwest Florida	World Woods (Rolling Oaks)
2006	Myrtle Beach, South Carolina	Grande Dunes
2007	Orlando, Florida	Lake Nona
2008	Innisbrook, Florida	Copperhead
2009	Sarasota, Florida	The Concession
2010	Naples, Florida	Olde Florida

As you can see from the above, our group is getting less adventurous, staying a little closer to home. We've also been playing fewer tournament rounds of late. One lesson about a golf group that remains together for over a decade also applies to everything else in life: Over a period of 13 years, everyone gets 13 years older.

In our group, the ages now range from 63 to 83. We have members who've had heart bypasses, heart valve replacements, pacemakers, bilateral knee replacements, Lasik eye surgery, and eye pressure surgery, not to mention the common chronic ailments, such as arthritis and diabetes, from which some of us suffer. But we're still growing strong.

Golf is a game for life, or at least for most of your life. Take time to enjoy it with your friends.

If you're still working, a golf road trip is one way you can get a taste of the joys of retirement early. Put together a golf group, pick a location and go play. With luck, this will turn into an annual event that will continue for many years to come.

CHAPTER 28

RULES FOR A GOLF TRIP COMPETITION

Someone who understands that the word "fair"
only applies to weather needs to be in charge.
— *The Patrick Golf Group*

An essential component of any good golf trip, or any single round, is a reasonably "fair" competition. And any good competition requires the transfer of money from the losers to the winners. (I have always believed that the exchange of a small amount of money is much better than the exchange of a large amount.)

In addition, any multi-round event needs to have a Champion who is justly rewarded for his hard fought and hard earned victory.

Over our 13 years of annual golf trips, our group has developed the set of rules, including those for payments, and pairings set out below. We've found them to result in a fun seven-round tournament with eight participants. Changing the handicap every day keeps everyone in the hunt and keeps the competition exciting and maybe even "fair." You may want to use them as is or as a starting point as you prepare for your first, or your next, group golf trip.

THE PATRICK GROUP GOLF RULES

1. These rules apply to the Seven Official Competitions described herein. On all other occasions, participants are permitted to make any other arrangements or wagers they wish under the "consenting adults" rules.

2. Pairings will be made according to the attached Official Pairing list.

3. Each 18-hole scheduled event will consist of the following three separate contests: a singles event, a better-ball-of-two event and a best-two-balls-of-four event.

   The singles event will be decided by net total score of the winning participant versus all others.

   The better-ball-of-two event will be decided by the best net ball of the winning twosome versus the other three twosomes.

   The best-two-balls-of-four event will be decided by the best two net balls of the winning foursome versus the other foursome.

4. Each participant will pay a tournament fee of $330 U.S. in advance to the banker.

5. Daily winners will be paid at the end of each day's play as follows:

Singles (per man)   First $70 Second $50
Third $20

Better-ball-of-two First $80 Second $40

(per twosome)

Best-two-balls-of-four (per foursome) First $60

6. The overall event winner will be determined
    by the total points accumulated from play in
    all three events. Points will be accumulated
    daily per player as follows:

    Singles   Winner 8 points, Second
                     7 points..... Last 1 point

    Better Ball   Winner 4 points, Second
                     3 points, Third 2 points, Last
                     1 point

    Best Two Balls Winner 2 points, Loser 1 point

7. All ties will be broken on the cards starting in
    the following manner:

                A. Lower net back nine

                B. Lower net total Holes 13-18

                C. Lower net total Holes 16-18

                D. Lower net score on Hole 18

    If a tie remains, cards will be matched in a
    sudden-death manner starting with the #1
    handicap hole.

8. The overall event winner pool will be paid
    out at the end of the tournament as follows:

First Place $180, Second Place $75, Third Place $45

In addition, the overall Champion will receive a print suitable for framing, worth approximately $100, from one of the courses played during the trip.

9. All play will be conducted under the official USGA Rules of Golf, including the 14-Club Rule, with the following exceptions:

    To be counted, any putt must be holed out – no exceptions.

    Each player will be limited to a maximum NET double bogey on any hole. For example, on a par four, a player with no stroke cannot record more than a six, and a person with a stroke cannot record more than a seven.

10. Any ball hit out of bounds or lost during play will be considered to be in a lateral hazard with a one-stroke penalty. The next shot will be played two club lengths from the assumed point of entry.

11. Official USGA handicaps will be used to determine the *initial* handicap for each player for the first round of the tournament.

12. For subsequent rounds, the handicap will be adjusted as per the table below utilizing the maximum NET double bogey rule.

Current day's NET score using current day's handicap	Next day handicap adjustment versus par
1-3(73-75)	+ or – 1
4-6(76-78)	+ or – 2
7-9(79-81)	+ or – 3
>10(>82)	+ or – 4

1. Any disputes, as well as any decisions not made clear by the above, will be resolved by the Committee.

OFFICIAL PAIRINGS

Participants

1. Tom

2. Ken

3. Ray

4. Lindsey

5. Mike

6. Dave

7. David

8. Jim

Sample Pairings

Round	Team 1 vs. Team 2		Team 3 vs. Team 4	
1. Castle Rock	1 + 6	2 + 5	3 + 8	4 + 7
2. Port Stewart	2 + 3	5 + 8	1 + 4	6 + 7
3. Port Rush	1 + 8	3 + 6	2 + 7	4 + 5
4. Royal Dublin	1 + 2	3 + 4	5 + 6	7 + 8
5. Olde Head	1 + 7	2 + 8	3 + 5	4 + 6
6. Waterville	2 + 6	3 + 7	1 + 5	4 + 8
7. Ballybunion	2 + 4	6 + 8	1 + 3	5 + 7

You can download a score sheet for this format at my web site www.thegolobetrottinggolfer.com.

SECTION FOUR

TRAVEL: THE OTHER REASON TO RETIRE

*He who returns from a journey is not the same as he
who left.*
— Chinese Proverb

*Twenty years from now you will be more disappoint-
ed by the things that you didn't do than by the ones
you did do. So throw off the bowlines. Sail away from
the safe harbor. Catch the trade winds in your sails.
Explore. Dream. Discover.*
— Mark Twain

CHAPTER 29

WHERE IN THE WORLD SHOULD WE GO?

*Everyone should take the time to prepare his
or her "bucket list."
Then set your priorities and begin to empty the
bucket.*

— Dave

In 2007, Jack Nicholson and Morgan Freeman co-starred in a buddy movie that struck a strong chord with many middle-aged Americans, including me. In "The Bucket List," they play two terminally ill cancer patients who meet at the hospital where they're receiving treatment. Recognizing that their time is limited, they check out against medical advice so that they can live their last days to the fullest. To prepare themselves, they create a "bucket list" of things they want to see or do before they kick the bucket. The concept had such broad appeal that the term immediately became a common expression. If you missed the movie, rent it. If you caught it, watch it again. It's funny and poignant and full of wisdom that will help you plan your retirement, especially the travel part.

My wife and I started our bucket list before my retirement date arrived. After a week of working on it, Sue Ann decided to let me make the list and set the priorities, provided she retained absolute veto rights. This was a great solution and one that I've gotten used to in many areas of my life.

My original intention was to take a trip every quarter. Since I retired at 60, this would allow us to take 40 trips before reaching age 70. Statistically, we could both expect to be in Phase One – healthy and mobile – which would help assure that we could complete our bucket list.

My wife vetoed that plan. She declared that two trips a year would be enough and that no trip could last more than ten days. From time to time, I've gained a variance on the ten-day rule, and we've taken 17-day trips when the distance was especially far; but she hasn't budged on the limit of two trips per year.

In the past six years, we've stayed true to this plan. We've taken 12 trips and have two scheduled for later this year. We've been to most of the countries in Europe, to China and to the southern part of Africa. We've taken land tours, as well as cruises on large ships, small ships and river boats. We have traveled with small groups of friends, with one couple (including one we met on a previous cruise) and even by ourselves.

Before we retired, my wife and I had vacationed in Hawaii, cruised the Caribbean, cruised to and ridden trains through Alaska, and toured Southern Africa, including a safari that ranks as one of our top travel experiences.

We prefer to book a cruise or a tour, especially if we're headed for someplace exotic, like China or Russia. That way we have the benefit of professionals who know the area and the language, we can relax and let someone else take care of the arrangements, and we generally get good value for what we spend. (My golf group's experience in Cabo San Lucas, described in Chapter 27, demonstrates that the details of travel planning aren't my forte.) But we do have friends who have a wonderful time researching and planning an entire trip all by themselves.

I have found that the most important thing is to approach travel with the right attitude.

Every form of travel has its pluses and minuses. I have to warn you in advance, my scale always tilts to the pluses. When it comes to a trip of any kind, anywhere, I'm a very easy grader, because I LOVE TO TRAVEL!!!

In life there are glass-half-full and glass-half-empty folks. We all can spot who they are, and we know which we'd rather be around.

As you travel, you will be inconvenienced. You will have food that is barely acceptable or that you don't like. You may not find your favorite (or even a good) wine. You will be with some people who are loud and obnoxious. You will have to stand in line and wait. Some of your guides will be difficult to understand. Sometimes the toilet facilities and hotel rooms won't be up to your standards. Sometimes the weather will be bad, and the seas may be so rough that you get sick. I have experienced all of this and more.

BUT, in spite of all this, I have loved every trip. My wife and I have seen some amazing things: the Great Wall and twin baby pandas in China, the magnificent animals of Southern Africa, the palaces and churches of St. Petersburg, the castles along the Rhine, Kilauea Volcano on the Big Island of Hawaii, the Parthenon in Athens by night, everything in Rome, Saint Mark's Square in Venice, the cathedral in Toledo, Spain, and many more.

Also, on every trip we have either strengthened our relationships with the friends who accompanied us or met wonderful people to share our experiences.

None of the inconveniences of travel come close to matching the excitement of what you see and experience, especially for glass-half-full people. So don't be dismayed when you hear the glass-half-empty folks return from a trip and complain about the food, the weather, and the accommodations. Don't let their negative comments keep you from enjoying the wonderful sights that you can see and enjoy. Ignore the nay-sayers, and enjoy yourself.

Of course, good planning will help increase the pleasant experiences and reduce the inconveniences. The remaining chapters of this book will discuss what to expect from different travel options, as well as what I've learned (sometimes the hard way) about ways to get the most out of each of these. I've also thrown in some general travel tips. As examples, I've interwoven accounts of trips to some of my favorite destinations; ones well worth consideration for anyone's bucket list.

CHAPTER 30

START WAY BEFORE RETIRING

The world is a book, and those who do not travel
read only one page.
— Saint Augustine

For my wife and me, learning how to travel and exposing our children to the world at large started years before I retired. The little exercise on aging described in Chapter 3 alerted me to the reality of time. As we approached our forties, it was obvious to Sue Ann and me that we only had a few years before the kids would be grown and the opportunity to travel with them and expand their view of the world would be lost.

This was brought home to me in spades one holiday season when we took our son and daughter to see a Christmas show in downtown Columbus, Ohio, where they were amazed by the "big buildings." While Columbus in those days did have a dozen or so medium-sized buildings, it was no New York or Chicago.

So we undertook our initial travel to educate our children. We took most of these trips during their spring breaks, but we also worked in a few shorter ones over Thanksgiving and a couple of longer ones in the summer. In those days, the kids were busy with organized summer activities, but I felt that expanding their minds was more important than seeing that they showed up for every baseball game or swim meet.

Some of these family trips were targeted to be directly educational. One summer we drove to Philadelphia to see the places that played key roles in the formation of our great country. From there, we drove to Washington, D.C., to visit the monuments, the seats of government, the White House, Arlington National Cemetery and the wonderful museums that make up the Smithsonian. After a quick stop at Mount Vernon, we were off to the village of Williamsburg for a few days of witnessing what life was like in the eighteenth century. (We also visited the amusement park and the discount shopping mall.) This "Americana Tour" is an experience that all four of us remember fondly, although at the time it wore us out.

The primary purpose of some of our other family trips was fun. We chose Cancun primarily for the beaches, wind-surfing and parasailing. But even that trip had an educational component – the impressive and beautiful Mayan ruins at Tulum, which sit on a spectacular site overlooking the Caribbean. Tulum is a relatively small but well-preserved example of what the Mayans built more than a thousand of years ago.

This side trip proved more adventurous than we'd predicted. I learned that if the rental car guy wants to show you how to change a tire, you should pay attention, and that Spanish learned by an early first year 15-year-old daughter, rewarded with a grade of C, is not much help when a tire blows out in the middle of nowhere.

While we were in Hawaii enjoying the beaches, we also visited Pearl Harbor and the Polynesian Cultural Center, both on Oahu. We had fun exploring Maui, something that really must be done in late winter or early spring, when the whales are in residence. We drove to the top of Haleakala, the spectacular dormant volcano that rises from sea level to more than 10,000 feet. The view of the crater is supposed to be best at daybreak, but that timing didn't work for my family.

On our trip to Los Angeles and San Diego, we started at Universal Studios, visited the *Queen Mary* and the *Spruce Goose* in Long Beach and ended in La Jolla, a town as lovely as its name, which means "the jewel" in Spanish.

The trip that the kids liked best was a seven-day cruise of the Western Caribbean. Once my son found out that you could order free food brought to the room at any hour of the day or night, he never wanted to leave.

We also took a couple of Eastern Caribbean cruises with friends who had children about the same ages as ours. On the first of these, I insisted that we take a tour of each island. The second time, we simply enjoyed the beautiful beaches.

Finally, we spent one very memorable family Christmas at a small beach hotel on St. Thomas. The weather was wonderful, and seeing Santa on the beach in shorts was interesting, but it didn't feel like Christmas. The high point was spending Christmas Eve with friends who had a house on the small island of St. Johns only a five-mile ferry ride away. We watched at dusk as a sailboat entered the harbor lit with thousands of Christmas lights and carrying a steel drum band and a large Santa Claus. The band played and sang "This Is Your Santa Claus" to a driving Caribbean beat. Every child on the island lined up to receive a gift from Santa on the makeshift stage. It made for a Christmas Eve none of us will ever forget.

And, yes, Sue Ann and I did take the kids to see New York City and all the really tall buildings. We went to the outside observation deck on top of the World Trade Center. We will remember this always.

If your children are still living at home, I suggest that you take the opportunity NOW to make your own travel memories that everyone will enjoy forever. Time passes very quickly, and you can never replace the opportunities that you miss.

CHAPTER 31

TRAVEL TIPS

What is traveling? Changing your place? By no means!
Traveling is changing your opinions and your prejudices.
— *Anatole France*

Traveling with your children to expose them to different experiences is very important; and there is a time in life to do that before they get too busy and develop lives and schedules of their own. But traveling without your kids provides opportunities to deepen already close friendships, turn acquaintances into good friends (or otherwise) and make new friends. Over the years, my wife and I have done all of the above.

We've also come to agree with something Mark Twain once said: "There ain't no surer way to find out whether you like people or hate them than to travel with them."

One of the first decisions you have to make as you plan a trip, right up there with deciding where you want to go, is to decide whether you will go alone, with family, with another couple, with a group of friends or acquaintances or with an affinity group. By "affinity group," I mean a group in which you may not know any of the other individuals beforehand, but in which you all share a common interest. It could be a scuba trip organized by a dive shop or a cycling tour of the California wine country. In our case, it was a group of alumni and friends of a university.

For many folks, this decision can make or break a trip. In fact, the first time Sue Ann and I traveled alone, she was very concerned that she would have only me to talk to (not with) for the entire trip.

Since then, the most important thing that we have learned about traveling is that no matter where we have gone or what form of trip we've taken, we have always met fun and interesting people who also enjoy the experiences of traveling and making new friends. On a river cruise in Europe, we met a travel agent and her husband. The four of us hit it off so well that since then, we have traveled with them as part of a group she arranged for a river cruise in Portugal with a side trip to central Spain. We've even joined them for a fun weekend in Branson, Missouri. And we have already signed up for another group trip with them for next summer.

So don't be afraid to go by yourselves. There will be others looking to meet people also.

Over the course of many years of travel, I have developed a few specific tips that you may find useful as you plan your first or next adventure.

1.   I never purchase the Travel Protection Program (insurance) offered with all organized

trips. At eight to 10 per cent of the price of the entire trip, the cost is very high. A tour or cruise company's own cancellation policies normally allow for return of 50 percent or more if you cancel the trip more than a month before the scheduled departure date. Things do come up that will cause you to miss a trip; but if you plan to travel a lot and if you don't miss any scheduled departure dates, your tenth trip will essentially be free, compared to what you would have paid if you'd insured each trip through the Travel Protection Program.

2.   To cover serious medical emergencies that could occur while on a pleasure trip, or any time I am more that 150 miles away from home in or out of the United States, I have purchased a policy that covers medical referrals and air medical evacuation back to my home city if necessary. I bought this Medjet Assist policy through a travel agent. The cost for my wife and me for three years was $1,380.

3.   When traveling to a country that does not use the U.S. dollar, I never change money at the counters in the airports. These money changing businesses charge very high fees. Today most of the world is full of ATM's, which do not charge exorbitant fees. Just make sure your card will work in ATM's outside the U.S. I also always take some dollars with me. At many tourist venues, some merchants accept American currency, but they

may charge rates higher than that country's banks.

4. I've found that the best way to get rid of foreign currency as you head back to the U.S. is to use it to pay part of your last hotel or cruise ship bill.

5. Call your credit card company and let them know where you will be traveling and when you will be there. This may prevent your card being declined by your provider for security reasons, especially if you don't travel very often.

6. Call your cell phone company to get your phone authorized in your destination country, or purchase a separate phone for use outside the U.S. I found that I was able to buy a separate phone with the same number for use in Europe for only $10 more than the cost to authorize my phone for only one visit. Either way, you need to be aware of the charge per minute overseas, which can be quite expensive.

7. These days, it's cheaper and easier to maintain contact via the Internet. All ships and most hotels have computers that can be used to access your computer mail box. It is likely that there will be a small charge for this service. Recently, many ships have added Wi-Fi service at no cost so you can use your own computer for free. Many cities also have Internet cafes where you can use a computer very cheaply or even a McDonald's,

where you can connect for free via your laptop. Shopping malls and public parks throughout Europe now have Wi-Fi zones, where Internet access is also gratis. And by using the Internet, you also won't be waking your friends and family members in the middle of the night when you're seven time zones away.

8. While we are on the topic of the Internet, a recent experience has shown us the value of putting your e-mail address on your bag tags as well as your phone number and address. While returning from a recent trip, our bags were sent to Naples, Italy, instead of to Naples, Florida. A couple of days later, Sue Ann found an e-mail from the Naples, Italy airport lost and found center in her SPAM file asking what they should do with these bags. Because of time differences it can be difficult to communicate via phone, but the Internet solved that problem, and we got our bags back.

9. Ask your doctor to write a prescription for antibiotics, and get it filled before you leave. My wife and I have found that a Z-Pack will take care of most things to which we have been exposed. Getting sick overseas can turn a trip into a nightmare, and you won't want to waste a day trying to find, and get an appointment with, an English-speaking doctor.

10. Every morning before you head out for sightseeing, take a photo of the itinerary or something with the day's location. That way, when you get home, you'll be able to tell where your pictures were taken just by looking at your camera.

11. When I visit especially historic or beautiful places, I purchase a small book containing both pictures and writing. The photos are much better than I can take, and the words add context and history to the subject. These modestly priced books are readily available in English and many other languages at most significant locations.

12. I always ask someone on a trip to use my camera to take a few pictures of me and my wife or our group in front of the most famous landmark or vista. When we get back, I have a 4 x 6 print made. We frame and display these around our home as mementos of our trips and what we saw.

13. I also edit our pictures and store them on a CD in case family or friends want to see what they can expect from a future trip of their own.

14. We do not bring home many gifts for friends and family. We see lots of people shopping for such gifts, which are a waste of time and money. How many of you have received gifts from somewhere you have never been that have no meaning to you? What's the point? Sharing your pictures via the Internet

is much easier and probably a little more meaningful to family and friends.

15. On each trip, we do purchase a Christmas ornament. This is not expensive but is a great reminder of our travels as we decorate our tree each Christmas season.

16. Take advantage of pre-tour or cruise extensions if offered. These two- or three-day introductions are keyed to a more relaxed pace than the main tours; they give you an opportunity to adjust to the change in time zones, as well as to see additional venues.

17. Traveling can be very busy and tiring. While I love to go on an excursion every day, my wife likes to take a day off after six or seven days of sightseeing. Take a look at the schedule and see if there is something you wouldn't mind missing.

CHAPTER 32

MAKING THE MOST OF CRUISING

Some cruise to relax.
I cruise to learn, to meet people and to have fun.
— Dave

Cruising is a great way to have fun, to meet compatible people and to experience different places and things. It also is hands-down the most convenient way to see the world. Once you're on board the ship, you unpack only once. And if you're fortunate enough to live within driving distance of a cruise port offering itineraries to places you want to go, you won't even have to endure the hassles of 21st century air travel. But, like most thing in life, having a great cruise experience involves making the right choices and planning carefully.

The first choice is where to go. This seems obvious, but it should be determined by what you hope to accomplish. Or maybe you do not want to accomplish anything. That's okay also.

For example, if you want fun in the sun, the Caribbean is your best bet. If you want to visit the capitals of the world and experience different cultures, a Scandinavian cruise or a riverboat cruise through Europe are good choices. For visiting different cultures in a relaxed atmosphere, cruises of the Mediterranean are hard to beat.

Also important is the time of year to travel. I always use the Internet to check temperature ranges and average rainfall at the ports of call. That way, for example, you can avoid encountering monsoons during the rainy season at what would be a tropical paradise a few months later. And prices can vary greatly depending on the season and the length of the cruise.

Generally, the longer the cruise, the lower the price per person per day; and holidays, when demand is high, can be especially expensive. Repositioning cruises, where a cruise line moves a ship from its summer to its winter home port, and vice versa, are real bargains. When friends of ours took a 14-day repositioning cruise from Galveston to Barcelona on Royal Caribbean's *Voyager of the Seas,* they paid about $65 per person per day for a spacious outside cabin. They had such a good time that they tried to book a seven-day Western Caribbean cruise with similar accommodations on the same ship over the week between Christmas and New Year's and were quoted a price three times as much per day. They opted instead for the same itinerary in February, paying not quite twice the price of the repositioning cruise for the same cabin.

The next matter you'll need to address is how much you want to spend and how formal or informal you want to be on board the ship. Cruises are all-inclusive vacations: While you're on board, your accommodations, meals (including room service but not including alcohol and sometimes specialty restaurants), fitness and sports facilities, swimming pools and hot tubs, and entertainment are part of the basic price. That can make cruises remarkably good values. However, you are not allowed to bring wine, beer, liquor or even sodas or bottled water with you; and with drink prices similar to those in hotels, a bar tab can add up to a rude surprise when you disembark. For that matter, so can the oh-so-tempting spa services, the casino and the fees for Internet connections. A cruse ship can be a pricey place to spend an hour a day surfing the web.

Sue Ann and I have tended to choose mid-priced and rather informal cruises. With this approach, we have found the food to be good and plentiful but not always great. The waiters and cabin service have been outstanding, since these folks work for tips and their pay depends on how passengers rate them at the end. The nightly live entertainment has varied some in quality but has almost always been enjoyable.

Depending on the home port and itinerary, ships of different sizes will be available. We have traveled the Caribbean, Alaska and Scandinavia on large ships carrying 2000 to 2700 passengers. We recently toured the Mediterranean on a medium-sized ship with about 700 passengers. Our two other Mediterranean cruises have been on small ships with as few as 150 passengers. We have also enjoyed two river cruises on ships with only 125 to 150 passengers.

Even when they're big, today's cruise ships tend to be so well-designed that once on board you won't get the sense that you're confined on a vessel with thousands of fellow passengers. The larger ships do generally have better evening entertainment, more options for dining and a larger choice of off-ship tours and activities. The small ships have a more intimate feel and provide the opportunity to interact with all the passengers and the crew.

Once you choose a cruise and a ship, you will need to pick your cabin. The choices on the larger ships are inside or outside cabin (sometimes with or without balcony), deck level from low to high and location on the deck level from front to rear. The inside cabins (no outside windows} are the cheapest, as are the cabins on the lower decks.

My philosophy is that cabins are for sleeping, getting ready for dinner, dressing in the morning and, hopefully, some romance. Other than these activities, you should not spend a minute in your cabin; there is just too much to do elsewhere on the ship. Unless you splurge on a suite, most ship cabins are about the same size: adequate but small.

For your first cruise, I would suggest an outside cabin on the lowest deck in the middle of the ship. If you are concerned about sea sickness, this is the place to be, since it's the most stable; and the cost will be much lower than the same floor plan on the higher decks. Most modern cruise ships are equipped with gyroscope-controlled stabilizers. These are basically underwater wings that extend outward from the ship and rotate when the ship is underway to minimize the rocking and tilting. During our travels, we have experienced some sense of movement but not enough to cause motion sickness in anyone that we knew.

While on a ship, I always try to use the stairs when moving between the decks. This practice partially offsets my invariable overeating, and it also keeps me from having to wait for an elevator, which can be a problem on a 2000-passenger ship. This is just another reason for choosing a cabin on a lower deck.

To insure that your choices of the time of travel and cabin level are available, book your cruise at least six months in advance. I have used travel agents but have found it just as easy to book directly online with the cruise line. By booking early, at least in these difficult economic times, you should be able to take advantage of early booking savings and free offers, such as onboard credit for those little extras like a massage at the spa or wine with dinner.

Another decision is when to eat dinner. On larger ships there are usually two seatings in the main dining room, which is a white-tablecloth restaurant. My wife and I differ on this choice. I prefer the early seating so that we can enjoy the entertainment after dinner. My wife takes a little longer to dress for the evening, so she prefers the later seating. As a result of this disagreement, we have reached a compromise of sorts, and now we always take the later seating. (Most of the larger ships offer the same live shows twice, so that both early and late seating passengers can catch the act.) Whether you decide on the early or late seating, after dinner there will be live performances and movies to see, lounges for drinking and dancing, shops for spending and usually a casino for gambling.

On a medium-size or large ship, you'll also have the option of eating at a more informal buffet or bistro or ordering room service. But choosing the main dining room at least most evenings offers a better opportunity to meet people. Another choice to be made is whether you want to be seated at a small, medium or large table. You will likely be assigned to a table for the first night, but you can always change. We like a large table, say for ten or 12. This will allow you to move around the table during the trip and get to know more of your fellow travelers. At a table for four, you will be with the same people every night for the entire cruise. Even if you travel with another couple or some of your family, a little variety of company can be enjoyable.

Your ship may also have specialty restaurants that require a separate reservation, possibly with an additional food charge. If you want to try something different one night, you will need to make a reservation as soon as you get on the boat. These reservations generally get taken fast.

Another key decision is choosing your off-board and on-board activities. Choosing shore excursions is something that you need to do before the cruise, if you can, or at least as soon as you get on board the ship. The best activities can get sold out quickly; and certain specialized ones, such as scuba diving packages, may be cancelled if not enough people sign up ahead of time.

I like to choose one off-ship activity offered by the cruise line for every day the ship is in a port. Much of the time, guided tours of the local area will be among the options. These guided tours provide the history and context of the area's significant sights and the local people. The activities and tours arranged by the cruise line are usually well done, and in the unlikely event that something happens to delay your return, the ship will wait. If you decide instead, for instance, to rent a car and explore on your own and you have a flat, you may experience the unforget-table sight of your ship pulling away from the dock.

The alternatives to on-shore activities provid-ed by the cruise line are to hire a private guide in the port, take a taxi, or just get off the ship and walk around on your own; but if you take these options, allow yourself a good margin of time so that you're sure to be back aboard before the scheduled sailing. You can also simply stay on the ship and utilize the pool, the exercise facilities or the spa, which will often offer reduced rates for services during port days. Or you can simply relax and read a good book.

Massages and other on-board spa treatments get sold out very fast, especially for the preferred days and times. The best days for spa treatments are the days at sea if there are any on the itinerary. Unless you opt to stay aboard, attempting to get one of these spa treatments on days when your ship is in a port can rush other activities and turn what should be a relaxing experience into a hassle. The key is to check the itinerary, make your choices and sign up as soon as you board the ship.

The alternative to booking a cruise well in advance is to set aside some time on the calendar for a cruise and take advantage of last-minute deals on cruises that are not sold out. For example, at the current time the following savings are available on cruises with the lead times shown below:

LOCATION	LEAD TIME	DISCOUNT
Mexico	6 weeks	54 %
Caribbean	2 weeks	80 %
Panama Canal	13 weeks	50 %
Asia	12 weeks	59 %

There are several discount Internet cruise sites that offer deals like those shown above. I happened to get these off of the vacationstogo.com site.

My suggestion is that you plan your cruise at least one year in advance. This will provide time to do the research and make the decisions that will make your cruise most enjoyable. It will also allow you time to read up on the locations to be visited. For example, before cruising to Alaska, I recommend reading *Alaska: A Novel* by James A. Michener.

Don't wait. Start planning your cruise now.

CHAPTER 33

THE CARIBBEAN

*Its clear blue waters make many of its islands
popular vacation spots.*
*— The American Heritage® New Dictionary of Cultural
Literacy, Third Edition*

The above quote is certainly true. As pretty as some of the islands themselves may be, the true beauty of the Caribbean is the clear water, sometimes blue and sometimes light green. Any visit to the islands must include at least a day at one of the beautiful tropical beaches. They are among the best anywhere in the world.

There are many ways to visit the Caribbean, on large cruise ships, small cruise ships, on small chartered sailboats or by simply flying to an island and staying at a resort, condo or cottage. Our visits to the Caribbean have been made on very large cruise ships and by flying to a single island and staying put.

Our favorite way to enjoy the Caribbean is on a ship of any size. This method of travel provides a variety of excursion opportunities and allows you to visit several of the wonderful and different ports of call. If you want to see more than one island, this is the way to do it.

Because the Caribbean is right next door, getting to any single island is easy from most American cities – a couple of plane changes. But flying from one island to another too often involves flying to a hub – San Juan, Kingston or even Miami – to make connections. The process can eat up a whole day that you could be spending relaxing around the ship's pool.

Caribbean cruises are generally divided into eastern and western. The Western Caribbean ports of call include Jamaica, the Cayman Islands and the Caribbean coast of Mexico, Belize and Honduras, sometimes with a trip through the Panama Canal. Ships offering these itineraries sail from Galveston (near Houston), New Orleans, Miami and Tampa.

We prefer the cruises of the eastern islands. They are closer together and more diverse in size, topography and culture (some are English, others French or Spanish or even Dutch). The water is usually smoother in the eastern Caribbean, since the ships travel mainly on the leeward side of the islands.

The best way to start a cruise of the eastern Caribbean is to fly to San Juan, Puerto Rico. One good tip we have learned when cruising the Caribbean is to stay out of the Atlantic Ocean. If you start a cruise of the eastern Caribbean in either Miami or Fort Lauderdale, you may hit rough seas on the way to the islands, and even if you don't, you spend two days of your trip at sea.

Many of the cruises of the Caribbean are on the very large ships. Don't be afraid of these ships. They are very well organized; and since almost all ports-of-call have docks, getting off and on is easy. Ports without a dock require tendering (boating) to and from the ship, which wastes a lot of your precious onshore time.

Most of the Caribbean islands have great beaches. The best we've found is Orient Beach on the French side of the French/Dutch island of St. Martin/St. Maarten. The beach is a large, beautiful white sand crescent with the most gorgeous blue green water. Be aware that Orient Beach is clothing optional with a nudist colony at one end. The restaurants on the beach are very good; and I can report, after three trips and some careful study, that 100% of the men and 95% of women would look much better clothed.

Other favorite stops for us in the Caribbean include St. Thomas and St. John, two of the three U.S Virgin Islands. St. Thomas has great tourist shopping and some beautiful overlooks. It also has a pretty good golf course on the north side of the island. Mahogany Run Golf Course is public and is easy to reach by taxi from the cruise docks. The course is famous for its 13th, 14th and 15th holes, which are called the Devil's Triangle. These are a par 4, a par 3 and a par 5 built on a sheer cliff overlooking the Atlantic Ocean.

St. John is not to be missed. It is a very small island (about 10 miles long by about five miles wide) just five miles east of St. Thomas. St. John is accessible by a 20- or 30-minute ferry ride from the main harbor of St. Thomas's largest city, Charlotte Amalie. St. John boasts a world-famous resort at Caneel Bay, which was originally developed by the Rockefeller family. Most of the rest of the steep and hilly island and many of the beaches are protected as part of the U.S. National Park system. The main attractions of St. John are the beaches and the clear, shallow waters off Trunk Bay and Cinnamon Bay, which are great for snorkeling. Trunk Bay has been consistently voted one of the "Ten Best Beaches in the World" by *Condé Nast Traveler* magazine.

Another of my favorite islands is Grand Cayman in the western Caribbean. The major attractions of Grand Cayman are beautiful Seven-Mile Beach and the crystal-clear waters. Grand Cayman is one of the best scuba diving venues in the world. The water here is so clear that from a boat on the surface you can see the bottom 50 feet below. Only a few hundred yards off Seven Mile Beach is a sheer wall that drops vertically straight down to about 6000 feet.

Grand Cayman is a great place to try out scuba diving. Most cruise ships and resort hotels offer a two-hour introductory training program that will allow you to sample scuba diving down to about 30 feet, accompanied by an instructor. Diving is relatively safe at this level, and the experience is worth the small risk.

Grand Cayman also features an experience that I have seen nowhere else in the world. Accessible only by boat, Stingray City is a sand flat in the middle of a shallow sound. There you can walk, and snorkel, with stingrays and even have them literally eating out of your hand. Because these rays are used to being fed morsels of squid by humans, they are very friendly. They only part of them that can hurt you is the barb at the tip of their tail, and then only if you step on them when they're buried in the sand.

On Grand Cayman's northwest shore in the village of Boatswain's Bay is a sea turtle farm. In 1503, Christopher Columbus first named the three islands that later became known as the Caymans "Las Tortugas" because of the large number of sea turtles in the area. This farm, which can be toured, breeds the sea turtles to make sure there will be many in the waters for years to come. Some island restaurants serve this farm-raised turtle, but U.S. law forbids bringing back any products from sea turtles, which are endangered in the wild.

If your Western Caribbean cruise takes you to the eastern coast of Mexico's Yucatan Peninsula, don't miss the Mayan ruins. In addition to Tulum, which I described in Chapter 30, the impressive sites at Chichen Itza and Coba are likely to be among your ship's excursion options.

In addition to the experiences mentioned above, many islands offer a wide variety of special-interest tours, from raft trips on jungle rivers to shopping excursions to local straw markets and duty-free shops. Most islands feature all sorts of water sports, including parasailing, windsurfing (difficult, at least for me), jet skiing and even sailboat racing on an America's Cup 12-meter yacht. I have also enjoyed the Jolly Roger rum cruises (cocktails and dancing on sailing ships done up as pirate boats) and the submarine rides, that allow you to admire the colorful life of the underwater reef without getting wet.

The Caribbean is a great way to start your cruising experiences and have a lot of fun. Ports of departure are easy to reach from any city in America, and English and U.S. dollars can be used almost everywhere. I recommend a Caribbean cruise as way to learn how to make the most of future cruises and travel. Enjoy!!!

CHAPTER 34

THE MEDITERRANEAN

*With a unique combination of pleasant climate,
beautiful coastline, rich history and diverse culture,
the Mediterranean region is the most popular tourist
destination in the world.*

— Wikipedia

My wife and I have enjoyed three cruises in the Mediterranean Sea. All of our trips thus far have been around the northern Mediterranean coast. The first was on a small cruise ship that held about 150 people. The trip started in Barcelona, Spain, and ended in Rome, Italy.

We had been to Barcelona before, so we arrived two days early to see and enjoy more of this marvelous city. With a population of 1.6 million, Barcelona is Spain's second largest city. Not to be missed in Barcelona are the remarkable works of architect Antoni Gaudí, which can be seen throughout the city. Displaying an utterly unique imagination that delighted and shocked the world, his incorporation of flowing lines, detailed mosaics and even fanciful animals and plants gave energy and inspiration to the turn-of-the-century style known as Modernism. Gaudí was active between 1875 and 1925. His best known work is the immense but still unfinished Church of the Sagrada Família, the masterpiece he was creating at the time he was run over by a streetcar and died. This landmark has been under construction since 1882 and is financed only by private donations. When we were there, we were told that completion is planned for 2026, which will be the one hundredth anniversary of Gaudí's death.

Another unique Gaudí project is the Park Güell garden complex situated on the hill of El Carmel. Built in the years 1900 to 1914, this was originally part of a commercially unsuccessful housing development. The buildings flanking the entrance, like all of Gaudí's work, are highly original with fantastically shaped roofs and unusual pinnacles. This park is well worth your time to visit.

Other famous Gaudí buildings include the Casa Batlló. The local name for the building is the "House of Bones," because it does have a visceral, skeletal organic quality. It was originally designed for an upper-class family in a prosperous district of Barcelona.

Running through the center of Barcelona is its most famous street, La Rambla, which is popular with both tourists and locals alike. Its long, tree-lined pedestrian mall connects the center of the shopping area of the city with the Christopher Columbus monument at the city's port. This is a wonderful street for viewing the flowers, fruits, vegetables and even birds and animals that are for sale, as well as for enjoy-ing the local street performers. There are also many outdoor restaurants for a meal or for resting your feet over a cup of coffee or a drink.

One evening while in Barcelona, we enjoyed a dinner flamenco dance show. The food was good, the Spanish wine was very good, and the dancing was fantastic. One item to note is that restaurants in Spain generally do not open until 9:00 p.m. and do not get busy until 10:00 at the earliest.

After sailing from Barcelona, our first port of call was Minorca, a small Spanish island with a popula-tion of about 90,000. We bused to a resort area and enjoyed a quiet day on the beach.

Our next stop was at Minorca's sister island in the Ballerics, Mallorca (sometimes spelled Majorca) or "the larger island." The biggest city on Mallorca and the regional capital is Palma de Mallorca with a population of more than 500,000. Palma also serves as the port for Mallorca and has beautiful beaches and one of the largest private boat harbors in the Mediterranean. Members of the Spanish Royal Family traditionally spend their summer holidays in Mallorca in the Marivent Palace.

Palma is famous for its vast cathedral built on the site of a previous mosque. Although construction began in 1229, it was not completed until 1601. The beautiful "Park of the Sea" is situated just south of the great cathedral.

The Old City of Palma (just southeast of the cathedral) is a fascinating maze of streets built during the city's Arab past. The walkways of this quarter are fairly narrow, quiet streets surrounded by a diverse range of interesting buildings.

Our following day was spent at sea. These days-at-sea are great for relaxing, reading and getting a massage. On this particular day, the Mediterranean was literally a "sheet of glass" without even a ripple. It was surreal.

Our next port-of-call was Alghero on the Italian island of Sardinia. Sardinia is the second largest island in the Mediterranean. Alghero is a small city with only about 40,000 residents. The main attractions are some ruins from 1500 B.C. and the town's cathedral.

Porto Vecchio on the French island of Corsica was our next stop. Corsica, the most mountainous Mediterranean island, is located just seven miles north of the island of Sardinia. Porto Vecchio is a small tourist town with a full-time population of only 13,000 that swells to 50,000 during the summer months. The main attractions for the tourists are the island's beautiful beaches and its harbor for small boats.

Day Six of this cruise brought us to Livorno, Italy, which serves as the port of entry for the Tuscany region. Our cruise offered several tours for the day in port, including trips to Cinque Terre along the coast to the north, to Pisa with its leaning tower, to Lucca with its old city and shopping, and to Florence with its beautiful buildings filled with amazing works of art, over an hour away by bus to the east.

This was our first trip to Tuscany; and we knew we'd be back, so we chose the tour to Lucca, because the trip to Florence seemed too long. However, if you do not plan to return to Tuscany, you must take the tour to Florence.

Our final stop and the debarkation point for the cruise was Civitavecchia, Italy, the port that serves Rome 50 miles away. Rather than fly back home immediately, we had booked a hotel room in Rome for four nights, so that we could see this wonderful city. The hotel had arranged for a private guide for the next three days. My wife and I still agree that this was the best three days of touring that we have had to date.

Rome is the capital of Italy, with a metropolitan population of 3.5 million. Called the Eternal City, it is one of the world's richest in history and art and one of the world's great cultural, religious and intellectual centers.

The first of our three days in Rome was spent exploring the ancient city. Any tour of ancient Rome must start at the Forum. It is the central area around which classical Roman civilization developed. Construction on the site began more than 600 years before the birth of Christ. The oldest and most important structures of the ancient city are located in the Forum, including ancient Rome's royal residence and the surrounding Temple of the Vestal Virgins.

The Forum area served as a city square and central hub where the people of Rome gathered for justice and faith. It was also the economic hub of the city and considered to be the center of the Republic and the entire Empire. Even though the Forum is in ruins, enough is still standing or has been restored that one cannot help but be impressed with the size and beauty of the structures that were built more than 2500 years ago.

Near the Forum is the equally famous and impressive Roman Coliseum. The Coliseum is an elliptical amphitheatre and the largest amphitheatre ever built in the Roman Empire. It is one of the greatest works of Roman architecture.

Occupying a site just east of the Roman Forum, the Coliseum began construction between 70 and 72 A.D. and was completed in 80 A.D. Capable of seating 50,000 spectators, it was used for gladiatorial contests and public spectacles such as mock naval battles, animal hunts, executions, re-enactments of famous military victories, and dramas based on classical mythology. It remains a very impressive site even by today's standards.

Although they are less famous than the Forum or the Coliseum, the ruins of the Baths of Caracalla are worth a visit. These Roman public baths were built between 212 and 216 A.D. and remained in use until the Sixth Century when, the complex was sacked during the Gothic War. The bath complex covers approximately 33 acres. The main bath building was 750 feet long, 380 feet wide and 125 feet high and could hold an estimated 1,600 bathers. The ruins are in good shape, and it is impressive to learn how the plumbing and heating system for the baths functioned.

Our fourth stop during our tour of ancient Rome was at one of the most amazing buildings ever built, especially considering that it was built almost 2,000 years ago. The amazing building is the Pantheon, which is a circular structure with a coffered, concrete dome and a central 30-foot-diameter opening (oculus) to the sky. The dome is supported by 20-foot-thick walls. The Pantheon is 143 feet across and 143 feet high. Almost 2,000 years after it was built, the Pantheon still has the world's largest unreinforced concrete dome. It is also one of the best preserved of all ancient Roman buildings.

As a final treat on the first day, we visited a small section of the very old Appian Way, the road that connected the south of Italy to Rome. Anyone who took Latin in high school will remember the Appian Way.

Our second day was spent touring "newer" attractions of the city. Our first stop was at the fabulous Borghese Gallery. The Galleria Borghese houses a substantial part of the collection of paintings, sculpture and antiquities begun by Cardinal Borghese, the nephew of Pope Paul V. Built in the early 1600s, the Galleria Borghese includes 20 rooms on two floors. All of the rooms are decorated with fantastic painted ceilings and paintings by the best artists of the day, including Raphael, Rubens and Barocci. Many of the beautiful marble sculptures on display were commissioned for specific areas of the building. The largest number are works by Gian Lorenzo Bernini, which comprise a large percent of his lifetime output. Bernini's *Goat Amalthea with Infant Jupiter and Faun* (1615), his dynamic *Apollo and Daphne* (1622–25) and *David* (1623) are considered seminal works of baroque sculpture.

The Borghese Gallery should not be missed. Reservations are required. I strongly suggest that you hire a private guide to obtain the reservation and to help you enjoy and understand the significance of the paintings and sculptures on display.

Our next stop was Vatican City, which is a landlocked sovereign city-state whose territory consists of a walled enclave within the city of Rome. The Vatican, with an area of approximately 110 acres and a population of barely over 800, is the smallest country in the world.

Vatican City contains many buildings and attractions and is a very popular tourist destination. To avoid the long lines and to focus on the best of the many treasures, a private guide is a must.

Our visit to Vatican City started with the Vatican Museums, which are among the greatest museums in the world. Founded by Pope Julius II in the 16th century, the museums display works of art from the immense collection built up by the Roman Catholic Church throughout the centuries.

The Vatican Museums consist of 54 galleries. The treasures they house are many and varied. There is just so much to see. The last of the galleries is the famous and very beautiful Sistine Chapel. The Sistine Chapel is actually located in the Apostolic Palace, the official residence of the Pope. It is famous for its architecture and its decoration, which was frescoed throughout by the greatest Renaissance artists including Michelangelo, Raphael, Bernini and Botticelli. Michelangelo painted the 12,000-square-foot chapel ceiling between 1508 and 1512. He resented the commission, believing that his work would only serve the Pope's need for grandeur. However, today the ceiling, and especially *The Last Judgment,* is widely believed to be Michelangelo's crowning achievement in painting.

Outside the museums are the wonderful Vatican Gardens which cover about half of the entire area of Vatican City and are worth some of your time to enjoy.

Even though the Vatican Museums are wonderful, I thought that the most impressive parts of Vatican City were the very large and very beautiful St. Peter's Basilica and the impressive St. Peter's Square. St. Peter's Basilica covers 5.7 acres and can hold more than 60,000 people. The dome of St. Peter's rises to a total height of 448.1 feet from the floor of the basilica to the top of the external cross, making it the tallest dome in the world. Construction of the present basilica began in 1506 and was completed in 1626. Michelangelo worked on the construction for 18 years until his death in 1564. As a work of architecture, it is regarded as the greatest building of its age.

The interior decorations of the basilica are perhaps even more impressive than the sheer size of the building. Sculptures by Michelangelo, Bernini and others are among the many treasures inside.

To the east of the basilica is the renowned St. Peter's Square. Constructed between 1656 and 1667, the present square is the Baroque inspiration of Bernini. The square is actually laid out in two sections. The part nearest the basilica is a trapezoid; but rather than fanning out from the facade, it narrows. The second section of the piazza is a huge ellipse. The two distinct areas are framed by a Tuscan colonnade formed by doubled pairs of columns supporting a roof covered with statues. The part of the colonnade that is around the ellipse does not entirely encircle it, but reaches out in two arcs from the main entrance. In the center of the great square is a 130-foot-high Egyptian obelisk that is more than 3,000 years old.

Our third and final day in Rome started with a quick stop at the very large and impressive monument to Victor Emmanuel, the king who unified Italy in 1861. The white structure is 443 feet wide and 239 feet tall and was completed in 1935. It is clearly visible to most of the city of Rome. We were told that Victor Emmanuel's handlebar mustache is seven feet long and that a dinner for twelve was once held in the body of the horse on which he sits.

Our guide next took us to the town of Tivoli in the foothills about 20 miles east of Rome. Our first stop was the site of Hadrian's Villa, constructed as a retreat from Rome for the emperor in the early Second Century A.D. Hadrian's villa was a complex of more than 30 buildings, covering an area of 250 acres, much of which is still unexcavated. One of the most striking and best preserved parts of the villa is a pool surrounded by Corinthian columns and copies of famous Greek statues.

The real treat of our day in Tivoli was a visit to the beautiful Villa d'Este and its fabulous garden of fountains. Constructed for Cardinal d'Este in the 1550s, at the height of the Renaissance, around an earlier monastery on a steep hill overlooking Rome, the building is lavishly decorated with frescoes, reliefs and internal fountains. The most striking part of Villa d'Este, however, is its garden, a terraced extravaganza of shady trees and show-stopping fountains. The gardens are composed almost exclusively of water features utilizing some five hundred water jets in fountains, pools and troughs. Fountains of every description dazzle the onlooker, from the grand Fountain of the Dragons and the Wall of a Hundred Fountains to a miniature reproduction of Rome. The centerpiece is the gigantic Water Organ Fountain, which was still working and playing beautiful music while we were there.

Gravity supplies the water for all these fountains from the Aniene River, which is partly diverted through the town, a distance of almost a mile away. This is the most beautiful and amazing garden that I have ever seen.

Our second Mediterranean cruise, also on a small 150-passenger ship, started in Athens. Again, Sue Ann and I arrived three days early to get adjusted to the time change and to see Athens.

Athens is Greece's capital and largest city and one of the world's oldest cities, with a recorded history of around 3,400 years. The metropolitan region has a population of about four million.

The Parthenon is Athens' main attraction and one of the most recognized buildings in the world. It was built as a temple to the Greek goddess Athena, whom the people of Athens considered their protector.

Construction of the Parthenon began in 447 B.C. and was completed 15 years later. The temple is large, with a base of 228 feet by 101 feet and a height of 66 feet. The roof is supported by 46 Doric columns that are 6.2 feet in diameter. Much of the Parthenon has been restored, and it is truly beautiful.

The Parthenon sits on the Acropolis, a flat-topped rock that rises 490 feet above sea level over-looking the city of Athens. The surface area of the acropolis is only about 7.5 acres. In addition to the Parthenon, the Acropolis is home to ruins of several other temples and buildings. On the slopes and below the Acropolis are two theaters. The larger one built in 325 B.C. has a capacity of around 15,000. The newer one built in 161 A.D. can hold around 5,000.

At night the Acropolis is lit by spotlights and can be seen from almost anywhere in Athens. It is a truly beautiful sight.

While in Athens, we took a drive 43 miles south along the scenic coast to Cape Sounion, the site of ruins of an ancient Greek temple built in 440 B.C. in honor of Poseidon, the god of the sea. We also booked a day trip on a ferry that stopped at three of the many Greek Islands that lie in the Aegean Sea just out from Athens. The most famous of the three was the island of Hydra located 37 miles from Athens' port of Piraeus. A small island, Hydra has a population of fewer than 3,000. Most of them live in the main town, known simply as "Hydra port." It consists of a crescent-shaped harbor, around which is centered a strand of restaurants, shops, markets, and galleries that cater to tourists and locals. Steep stone streets lead up and outwards from the harbor area. Most of the local residences, as well as the hotels on the island, are located on these streets.

Laws forbid trucks, cars and motorcycles on Hydra. Donkeys, bicycles and water taxis provide the transportation. The inhabited area, however, is so compact that most people walk everywhere, although some tourists do take a ride on one of the many donkeys.

Back in Athens, we enjoyed a fun evening in the Plaka at a restaurant that featured Greek food, drink, singing and dancing. The Plaka is the picturesque old historical neighborhood, which is clustered around the northern and eastern slopes of the Acropolis.

We boarded our ship at Pireas to start our seven days of cruising. One of our fellow passenger couples learned a hard lesson of traveling as they were arriving to board the ship. Apparently an argument over the fare occurred as the taxi driver was in the process of unloading their luggage. To end the argument the driver slammed the trunk with the man's luggage still inside and took off never to be seen again. The lesson is to get your luggage out of the taxi before arguing about the fare.

Our first stop after leaving Athens was the port of Ermoupolis on the Greek island of Syros. Ermoupolis is a small town with a population of only 13,000. We took a bus ride around the island and a walking tour of the lovely old port.

The second stop was Navplion on the Greek Peloponnesian Peninsula. With a current population of only about 14,000, Navplion was the capital of Greece from 1829 to 1834. The main site here was a large castle built by the Venetians in about 1700 on a hill overlooking the harbor.

Next was Gythion, a town of 8,000 at the very southern tip of the Peloponnesian Peninsula. Our tour was actually to the medieval town of Mystras, which is just outside of the city of Sparta, about 35 miles inland from the port. Mystras was built on a steep hill in the Thirteenth Century but is still in fairly good condition with an active small convent.

Our fourth day was a restful day-at-sea as we cruised across the Ionian Sea to Italy.

Our first stop in Italy was at the port of Messina in Sicily. Messina is the third largest city on the island of Sicily. Its metropolitan area has a population of 500,000. Our tour destination was the village of Taormina, perched on a cliff overlooking the Ionian Sea. By far the most remarkable site at Taormina is the ancient Greek Theater, which is one of the most celebrated ruins in Sicily. But Taormina is actually a shopper's paradise. It has many old churches, lively bars, fine restaurants and a very large number of elegant shops selling beautiful Sicilian ceramics, gold and silver jewelry, antiques, high-fashion clothing and distinctive locally-made wrought-iron and marble furniture.

If your shopping dollars do not all get spent in Taormina, they will certainly be spent at our next stop, the remarkably beautiful Island of Capri, the "mother of all tourist towns." The island actually has two levels of shopping and restaurants. The lower level is the City of Capri, where most of the island's people live. The separate community of Anacapri, located high on the hills to the west, is the main tourist shopping area. You can get to Anacapri from Capri by taking a taxi or bus up the steep and winding road or by taking the funicular straight up the cliff. Anacapri is a good spot to enjoy a leisurely lunch in a restaurant with a beautiful view of the Mediterranean Sea and to sample the region's famous lemon liqueur, *limoncello*.

From Anacapri a ten-minute single-seat ski lift ride to the top of the island offers terrific views of the island, the Mediterranean Sea and even the volcano Mount Vesuvius to the northeast just outside Naples.

Anacapri is also noted for its handmade, expensive women's sandals. My wife bought one pair to take home with her and paid for another pair to be shipped back to the U.S. The second pair never arrived. This is the only time we have not received something we paid for overseas. Maybe this is why they insisted on being paid in cash instead of by a credit card. Beware!

While visiting the Isle of Capri, I suggest taking a boat ride from the main harbor to see the imposing Faraglioni, a formation of enormous rocks rising up out of the clear sea, and the famous Blue Grotto.

This cruise ended back at Civitavecchia, which as you will recall is the port for Rome. Did I mention earlier that we loved Rome?

Our third cruise of the Mediterranean began in Rome and ended 14 days later in Venice. We first headed north along the Italian coast, then east to Monte Carlo, then south and then east around the "boot" of Italy, east across the Ionian Sea, north to the Adriatic Sea's east coast, and finally west to Venice.

This time we booked a medium-size ship with about 680 passengers. We visited 12 ports, seven described earlier in this chapter. You may wonder why we booked a cruise to 12 ports if we have already been to seven of them. The answer is easy. We did that because we love visiting Italy, and we got to see five new ports.

Once again, we boarded in Civitavecchia. Our first stop was at Livorno, the port of entry to Tuscany. We liked our taste of Tuscany so much that we later returned for a trip described in Chapter 38 on land tours.

Our second stop was at Monte Carlo in the Principality of Monaco. Monaco, with a population of 33,000, is the second smallest country in the world, after Vatican City. Monaco is a narrow and hilly seaside principality that is totally surrounded by France.

Monte Carlo's famous Le Grand Casino is one of its most notable tourist attractions. The casino provided filming locations for the James Bond movies "Never Say Never Again," "Casino Royale" and "Golden Eye."

Monaco is known as a playground of the rich and famous. During our visit, the harbor was full of some of the largest private yachts in the world.

The next day, our port of call was La Spezia, Italy, home to a major Italian military and commercial harbor. The main reason for our stop here was to catch small ferry boats for trips to the various locations in the unique Cinque Terre region, a very steep and rugged portion of coastline with five small colorful, very picturesque villages. Over centuries, people have carefully built terraces right up to the cliffs that overlook the sea. Part of its charm is the lack of visible "modern" development. Hiking paths, trains and boats connect the villages, which cannot be reached by car. Cinque Terre is a very popular tourist destination.

Our final stop in northern Italy was Portofino, a small Italian fishing village and tourist resort on the Italian Riviera. The town of fewer than 1,000 residents is crowded around a small harbor. With its colorful three- and four-story buildings, Portofino is considered to be among the most beautiful Mediterranean ports.

The next two stops were Amalfi/Positano and Sorrento/Capri in southern Italy. In Sorrento my wife and I spent a magnificent day taking a cooking class in the home of one of the local merchants. The home, called Villa Ida, had been modified to allow about 20 people to cook and enjoy a pasta dinner. The meal, all prepared by the participants under the watchful eye of the grandmother of the family, consisted of mozzarella cheese on lemon leaves from their yard melted on a grill as the appetizer, a wonderful deep-fried eggplant lasagna, sliced potatoes cooked in white wine and tiramisu for desert. Of course, plenty of the local wine made the afternoon even more fun.

Our final port of call in Italy was Taormina in Sicily. Then our ship rounded the "boot" of Italy and headed for the Greek island of Corfu in the Ionian Sea. The town of Corfu has a population of about 30,000, while the population of the island is more than 100,000. While in Corfu we visited the palace of Achilleion on a hill six miles south of the city. This magnificent palace was built in 1890 by Empress Elisabeth of Austria, also known as Sissi, as a summer residence.

Taking Achilles as its central theme, the palace abounds with paintings and statues of this powerful figure from classical Greek mythology, depicting the heroic and tragic scenes of the Trojan War. The Imperial gardens include several beautiful classic Greek statues and provide a majestic view of the surrounding green hills, valleys and sea.

The next two ports-of-call were in countries that had until relatively recently been part of Yugoslavia. The first was Kotor in the small and relatively new independent country of Montenegro (population about 700,000). Kotor is a lovely small resort town of around 25,000 located near the end of the narrow Bay of Kotor. Rather than sightsee in Kotor, we spent our day visiting the inland town of Cetinje. We had an exceptionally knowledgeable guide on this trip, and I found the history of Montenegro very interesting.

What is today Montenegro was part of a much larger state that was overrun by the Ottoman Empire in 1499. The only part that remained independent was the relative small, mountainous territory between the Crnojević River and the Bay of Kotor which is the Montenegro of today.

Our guide told us that when the Ottomans would invade that territory, the local people would simply leave. After a couple of months, the Ottomans would have to leave because the area had no water and could not grow crops. It is a reasonably flat elevated plain that is full of rocks everywhere.

Located on the rocky plain, Cetinje has a population of fewer than 20,000. It is the site of the modest official residence of the king of Montenegro, Nikola I (1841-1921). This is another interesting story. Nikola I was the only king of Montenegro. He reined as prince from 1860 to 1910 and then as king from 1910 to 1918. According to our guide, he must have been an amazing man. Although king of a very small and very poor country he was hosted by and visited by most of the royalty of Europe.

In fact, for a number of years, the most important export from Montenegro was his daughters. Because of inbreeding, the blood lines in most of the European royal families were beginning to be plagued with genetic disorders. As a result, these families were looking for a different gene pool, and Nikola I and his daughters provided the answer. Five of his nine daughters were married to European princes and kings, giving Nikola the nickname "the father-in-law of Europe." Of course, the daughters made sure that Montenegro was supported as needed.

More recently, when Yugoslavia was dissolved in 1992, Montenegro affiliated with its neighbor to the east, Serbia. This was a somewhat difficult relationship; and in 2006 Montenegro voted, by a small majority, to become a fully independent country.

Our next port-of-call was the city of Dubrovnik in Croatia. Called the "Pearl of the Adriatic," Dubrovnik became an important Mediterranean Sea power in the Thirteenth Century. It is one of the most prominent tourist destinations on the Adriatic. The population of Dubrovnik is around 50,000.

Dubrovnik's Old City was built in the Thirteenth Century. The medieval Old City is laid out in an almost square shape and juts out into the Adriatic with water on two and half sides. Tall walls run 1.2 miles around the Old City. Although severely damaged by an earthquake in 1667, Dubrovnik managed to preserve its beautiful Gothic, Renaissance and Baroque churches, monasteries, palaces and fountains. The Old City is a maze of broad streets and many narrow alleys.

In 1991, Croatia and its neighbor to the north, Slovenia, declared their independence from Yugoslavia. Later that year, Dubrovnik was attacked by Yugoslavian forces from Serbia and Montenegro. The city was besieged for seven months, during which it was heavily damaged by shelling and bombing. Most of the buildings in the countryside outside the city were sacked and burned.

The beautiful Old City has been restored, but you can still see areas where buildings were hit by shell and bomb fragments. The Old City with its shops, restaurants and elegant old buildings is a delight to visit.

We started our visit to the Dubrovnik area by taking a bus tour of the countryside. While many of the farm houses and barns have new rebuilt tile roofs, we did see several burned-out buildings that remain from the 1991 invasion.

For me, the most memorable part of this bus tour occurred during our visit to the small seacoast town of Cavtat, located nine miles south of Dubrovnik. Cavtat is a very attractive resort with a large harbor. We visited it early in the morning when the temperature was unexpectedly cool. Our guide suggested that we stroll along the harbor promenade and enjoy a cup of coffee or hot chocolate by the church at the end of the walkway. After visiting the church, we took our guide's recommendation and stopped for hot chocolate. Well, this was not the hot chocolate that we get in the States; it was either melted chocolate bars or a thick chocolate soup. Whatever it was, it was wonderful and something I will never forget.

Our journey ended with a two-day stay on the ship while docked on the Grand Canal of Venice. Venice is as good as it gets for me, as you can tell from my description of this legendary city in the land tour chapter of this book (Chapter 38).

I hope that after reading this chapter you will see why the Mediterranean region is "the most popular tourist destination in the world," as Wikipedia points out. It is a must for any bucket list traveler.

CHAPTER 35

ALASKA

Seward was no dummy.

— *Dave*

On March 30, 1867, Secretary of State William H. Seward signed an agreement with the Russian Minister to the United States to purchase Alaska. The agreement, widely referred to as "Seward's Folly" (and the land popularly known as "Seward's Icebox"), ceded possession of the vast territory of Alaska to the United States for the sum of $7.2 million. This may well have been the deal of the Nineteenth Century.

Alaska, America's 49th state, is our largest and least densely populated. With a population of fewer than 700,000 people, it is more that twice as big as Texas, which ranks second in size.

Cruises to Alaska are popular because of the many and varied sights they offer. There is so much to see and do that between 40 and 50 tours were offered at each of our ports-of-call.

A cruise of the Inside Passage usually lasts about seven days. However, I would recommend booking the additional five-day land tour to Fairbanks through Denali National Park to see more of the varied and rugged Alaska landscape.

Our cruise started in Vancouver, British Columbia. Unfortunately, we didn't arrive in Vancouver in time to see the city on our own or take one of the tours that were available through the cruise line. From what I heard from those who did, it is a beautiful city, and we should have arrived a day earlier.

Our first day on board ship was spent relaxing while sailing north to the Inside Passage. This provided a good opportunity to explore the ship, have a relaxing massage and read a good book.

The Inside Passage of the Alaska Panhandle and British Columbia protects oceangoing vessels from the sometimes turbulent waters of the Pacific Ocean. The route threads between the mainland and the many small coastal islands in the area. The passage allows ships to avoid some of the bad weather in the open ocean, visit the isolated communities along the way and have close-up views of some of the world's most spectacular scenery. The Inside Passage is heavily traveled by cruise ships, freighters, tugs with tows, fishing craft and ships of the Alaska Marine Highway and BC Ferries systems.

The first port we reached was Ketchikan, Alaska. This small city, population about 8,000, is located on one of the islands in the Inside Passage. Ketchikan is known as both the Salmon Capital of the World and the Rain Capital of Alaska.

This was one of our trips with friends, in this case five other couples, and the guys decided to spend the morning of our day in Ketchikan salmon fishing. The fishing was not great that day, but one of the guys did catch one.

While the fishing was disappointing, the scenery was spectacular. The islands around our fishing spots were covered with large fir trees, which served as resting spots for the many bald eagles in the area. In fact, the white-headed bald eagles were so numerous that the firs looked like Christmas trees decorated with white ornaments.

We learned that, like us, the bald eagles were fishing for salmon and that salmon were the cause of most bald eagle deaths. Apparently, bald eagles can only release prey in their talons while standing on a hard surface. An eagle that grabs a fish too big for it to carry out of the water cannot let go and will drown.

We spent our afternoon in Ketchikan visiting and hanging out in the quaint old downtown.

Our next port was Juneau. Juneau has been the capital of Alaska since 1906. It is the only state capital in the United States that cannot be reached by land. Its 31,000 residents live in the shadow of steep mountains that rise to about 4,000 feet above sea level. On top of the mountains is the Mendenhall Glacier, which is easily visible from the city.

From the tour options, we selected a float plane trip from the Juneau harbor over lush forests, water-falls, snow-capped mountains and colorful glaciers to the remote Taku Glacier Lodge for a wonderful feast of freshly caught wild salmon.

Skagway was our third stop and the starting point for many of the thousands of would-be gold-miners on their 500-mile journey to the Canadian Klondike gold fields in the years following 1896. Skagway is currently home to fewer than 1,000 people, although the population during the Gold Rush reached 30,000.

My wife and some of the other ladies in our group chose to visit Jewell Gardens while in Skagway. The flowers there and around all the cities where we stopped were very large and very colorful. During the summer months, the flowers, and the people, get almost 24 hours of daylight and plenty of rain.

My helicopter trip to walk on a glacier was cancelled due to low cloud cover, so I chose to hike a small and relatively flat part of the famous Chilkoot Trail, which was how most of the miners reached the Klondike gold fields.

We spent the next two days onboard, cruising first through Glacier Bay and then College Fjord. It might seem that spending two days looking at glaciers would be boring, but once you see and hear your first dramatic calving of a large glacier, the experience becomes quite exciting, even mesmerizing.

We left the ship in Whittier, which is not far from Alaska's main city, Anchorage. Here we boarded a sightseeing train for Denali National Park and Mt. McKinley – at 20,329 feet above sea level, the highest peak in North America.

Our first stop on the train was in the small town of Talkeetna, with a population of fewer than 1,000. There wasn't much to see or do here, but it was a nice chance to stretch our legs. The next stop was at the Mt. McKinley Princess Wilderness Lodge, where we spent the night.

Day nine of the trip included a motor coach trip through Denali National Park to the Denali Princess Wilderness Lodge. That afternoon, my wife and I elected to take a six-passenger twin engine airplane to view the top of Mt. McKinley. The small plane we went up in was not pressurized, so we had to wear oxygen masks above 10,000 feet. It seems that I'd forgotten to mention this to my wife. There is nothing worse that getting the "I am going to kill you" glare from behind an oxygen mask at 20,000 feet.

The top of the mountain was a little cloudy, but we did get to see the summit of McKinley on the plane's radar. Again I got "the glare" from my wife. It was an interesting way to see the mountain and surrounding areas, and we were able to watch planes with skis landing other tourists on the mountain's glaciers below us.

That evening we attended the Denali dinner theater for some good food and rousing singing. After the show, our group decided to have a drink before bed at one of the outside bars. It was about 10:00 p.m. and bright as day, with the sun still high in the sky. A debate began to decide if we should stay up for awhile to see the sun set. Our waiter then told us that we would have to wait three weeks for sunset, so we went to bed.

The following morning, we took a half-day tour of Denali National Park. Denali means "the great one" in the local native language and refers to the mountain. Although the park area is 9,500 square miles, or over six million acres, it has only 15 miles of paved roads, so that was the extent of our tour.

Due to the short growing season, the vegetation that we saw in the park was small and sparse. We did see some small squirrels and one moose with two newborn calves. The main viewing was of Mt. McKinley and the other snow-covered peaks in the area. Other members of our group who took the full-day tour along some of the many gravel roads in the park reported seeing several large bears.

The last two days of this trip were spent in Fairbanks. There, we visited a gold mine and even panned for gold. Unfortunately, my wife panned up a small nugget. I say that this was unfortunate because I was then offered the opportunity to purchase a holder and chain on which to display this trophy. She proudly wore her prize to dinner that night, and I have not seen it since.

As a final activity, we took a very interesting sternwheeler river boat cruise that afternoon to see many of the local points of interest, including a sled-dog training school and a replica Indian village.

As we found out on the way home, Fairbanks is a long way from everywhere. Our flight to Seattle took almost four hours. To fly all the way across the U.S. from Seattle to New York takes only about one hour longer.

Alaska is a great place to visit. There is a lot to see and to experience. The weather can be cool and wet even in mid-summer, but do not let that keep you from taking this trip. As I suggested earlier, to make the experience even more meaningful, read *Alaska* by James Michener.

CHAPTER 36

SCANDINAVIAN CAPITALS

*Famous as the land of the midnight sun, unique
culture, and great city life, Scandinavia is truly a
unique part of Europe.*
— *The Scandinavian Tourist Board*

A Scandinavian or Baltic Sea cruise provides a great deal of diversity from topography to culture, language and architecture. This region is filled with palaces and other historic buildings, as well as museums.

Our cruise began in London, which is a little unusual for cruises of this area. I think our ship must have been repositioning. Amsterdam seems to be the most popular embarking and disembarking point for Scandinavian cruises. Either city offers nonstop air service to the U.S.

Our first stop was Oslo, which was founded in 1048. In addition to being Norway's capital, Oslo is its largest city with a metropolitan population of about 1.4 million residents. It is also the home of the Noble

Prizes that are given out every year to both deserving and questionable recipients.

The part of Oslo that we loved was the wonderful Vigeland Sculpture Park, which no visitor should miss. It is a part of Frogner Park, located two miles northwest of the city center. The sculpture park covers 80 acres and features 212 bronze and granite sculptures created by Gustav Vigeland, who worked on this project from 1906 until his death in 1943.

At the highest point in the park lies its most popular attraction, the Monolith. This massive sculpture towers 46 feet high and is composed of 121 carved granite human figures rising toward the sky. The Monolith represents man's desire to become closer with the spiritual and divine. It portrays a feeling of togetherness, because the figures embrace one another as they are carried up toward salvation.

Another attraction of the Vigeland Park is the 58 sculptures that reside along a 328-foot-long, 49-foot-wide walking bridge. All are clad in bronze and contribute to the "human condition" theme of the park. A final treat is the Fountain, which was fabricated from bronze and adorned with 60 individual bronze reliefs. Portraying children and skeletons in the arms of giant trees, the Fountain suggests that from death comes new life. On the ground surrounding the Fountain is a large mosaic laid in black and white granite.

Our second port-of-call was Warnemunde, Germany, a fishing village of fewer than 10,000 inhabitants. Here we boarded a train for a three-hour trip to Berlin for a tour dubbed the "20th Century Berlin Experience."

Berlin is the capital of Germany and its larg- est city, with a population of 3.4 million. Our tour of Berlin included visits to a remaining part of the infamous Berlin Wall, Checkpoint Charlie, a museum dedicated to the 1948 and 1949 Berlin Airlift, and the famous Brandenburg Gate.

The Brandenburg Gate serves as a symbol of both Berlin and Germany and was also a symbol used by the Nazi Party. Built from 1788 to 1791 as the main city gate, it saw the passing of Napoleon's troops in the early 1800s, survived the Allied bombings of World War II and became part of the Berlin Wall dividing East from West from August 1961 until late 1989.

The Brandenburg Gate served as a backdrop for President Ronald Reagan's historic June 12, 1987 speech, in which he challenged Mikhail Gorbachev, then the General Secretary of the Communist Party of the Soviet Union: "Mr. Gorbachev, tear down this wall!" and changed the world.

Our next stop was in Tallinn, Estonia. A small country with a total population of 1.3 million, Estonia was occupied by the Russians from the end of World War II until August 1991. Tallinn is the country's capi- tal and largest city, with a population of just over 400,000. The two old districts of the city are known as the Upper Town and the Lower Town. The Upper Town is the location of the old Estonian Royal Pal- ace, now the Parliament Building. Across the street is a beautiful Russian Orthodox Cathedral. The Lower Town is one of the best preserved old towns in Europe and the site of Tallinn's Town Hall. The figure of an old warrior called Old Thomas was put on top of the spire of the town hall in 1530 to serve as a weather vane, and it is still there showing the wind direction and serving as the symbol for the city.

The beautiful Kadriorg Palace is located 1.5 miles east of the city center. This was the former palace of Peter the Great of Russia and now houses the Art Museum of Estonia and the Estonian presidential residence. The palace grounds include a large and exceptionally beautiful formal garden.

Our tour guide in Tallinn was very good and a little unusual. Guides normally waste a considerable amount of time counting the number in the group to make sure no one gets lost or left behind. Our Estonian guide started the tour by saying that she was not good at counting and that the Estonian minimum standard for tour guides states that she only needs to return with 90 percent of the group and that, therefore, there would be no counting. As a result, no time was wasted and everybody stayed close together.

The next stop was St. Petersburg, Russia, where there is so much to see that most ships, including ours, stay in port two full days. In fact, even two days isn't enough. A stay that short will leave you with such a good impression of this beautiful city that you'll find yourself adding a second visit to your bucket list. At least, that's what happened to us.

St. Petersburg was founded by Tsar Peter I on May 27, 1703. It was the capital of the Russian Empire for more than 200 years, until the Russian Revolution of 1917, when the Soviets moved the seat of government to Moscow. St. Petersburg bore the name Petrograd from 1914 to 1924, when the Soviets renamed it Leningrad to honor the revolution's mastermind, Vladimir Lenin. After Moscow, St. Petersburg is Russia's second largest city, with 4.6 million inhabitants. In 1991, with the Soviet Union collapsing, 54 percent of the Russian people voted to restore the city's original name.

One of the highlights of any visit to St. Petersburg has to be the State Hermitage Museum of Art and Culture. The Hermitage is one of the largest and oldest museums in the world. It was founded in 1764 by Catherine the Great and has been open to the public since 1852. Its collections comprise nearly three million items, only a small fraction of which are on permanent display. The painting collection is the biggest in the world and includes works by Leonardo da Vinci, Raphael, Titian, Rembrandt, Rubens, Van Dyck and many French Impressionists. The Hermitage spreads across a complex of six historic buildings, including the Winter Palace, a former residence of the Russian Tsars. This museum is so large and popular that it must be seen with a guide.

One of the main sights of St. Petersburg is the unbelievably beautiful and colorful Church of the Savior on Spilled Blood, so named because Tsar Alexander II was assassinated on that site in March 1881. Construction of the church began in 1883 and was finally completed in 1907. Topping the structure are two gold and five white, green and blue onion domes.

Another "must see" for any visitor to St. Petersburg is the so-called Tsar's Village. Now part of the town of Pushkin, the Tsar's Village is located 16 miles south of the center of St. Petersburg and is home to two beautiful palaces that were residences of the Russian imperial family. The larger of the two is the beautiful blue, white and gold baroque Catherine Palace with the adjacent Catherine Park and its fabulous gardens. The current building is on the site of an original summer residence built by Catherine I of Russia in 1717. Empress Elizabeth had the residence rebuilt in 1752-56 into the wonderful 1,056-foot-long structure that remains today.

When the German forces retreated in January 1944 after the 872-day siege of Leningrad, they intentionally burned and gutted Catherine Palace, leaving only a roofless hollow shell. Fortunately, prior to the World War II, the Russian archivists had managed to document a fair amount of the contents, which proved of great importance in reconstructing the palace. The largest part of the reconstruction was completed in time for the Tercentenary of St. Petersburg in 2003.

The highlight of the building, which contains many lavish rooms, is the Amber Room. Amber is fossilized tree resin, usually yellow-orange-brown in color. This opulent room is decorated with over six tons of amber panels backed with gold leaf and mirrors. Due to its singular beauty, this room has sometimes been dubbed the Eighth Wonder of the World.

During World War II the Germans looted the Amber Room, taking with them the panels. Knowledge of the amber's whereabouts was lost in the chaos at the end of the war. Its fate remains a mystery, and the search continues.

In 1979 efforts began to rebuild the Amber Room. In 2003, after decades of work by Russian craftsmen, the restoration was completed.

The other palace located in the Tsar's Village is the lovely yellow and white neoclassical Alexander Palace with its adjacent Alexander Park. Built between 1792 and 1796 by Catherine the Great for her favorite grandson and future emperor Alexander I of Russia, the Alexander Palace is primarily known as the favored residence of the last Russian Emperor, Nicholas II, and his family.

Nicholas II abdicated the throne during the Russian Revolution, on March 15, 1917 (March 2 by the Julian calendar, which Russia then used). Thirteen days later he returned to the Alexander Palace. Bolsheviks held the Imperial family there under house arrest until they were moved on the morning of August 1, 1917 by train to Siberia. For decades, doubt surrounded their eventual fate, but DNA testing has verified that skeletal remains found in Yekaterinburg were those of Tsar Nicolas, his wife, children and valet, and the family's doctor and its cook.

A third opulent imperial residence, the Peterhof Palace, was built by Tsar Peter I in 1723. Located about 15 miles west of the center of St. Petersburg on the Bay of Finland, part of the Baltic Sea, the palace forms the centerpiece of a compound. Scattered around the extensive grounds are 30 buildings and pavilions and more than 100 sculptures. Many of these statues are gilded with gold leaf and incorporated into the gardens' magnificent fountains.

As one can easily see from these three unbelievably large, beautiful, ornate palaces, being a Russian royal was a great life until the revolution.

None of the other capitals of Scandinavia compares to St. Petersburg. St. Petersburg definitely needs to be on everyone's bucket list.

After St. Petersburg, the next stop for us was Helsinki. Helsinki is the capital and largest city in Finland, with a population of almost 600,000. It was difficult to be impressed with anything after St. Petersburg, but we did enjoy a visit to Helsinki's Seurasaari Open-Air Museum, located on a pretty green island. This museum was founded in 1909 and consists of more than 100 buildings representing the different provinces of Finland. Most of the structures are wooden agrarian buildings from the 18th and 19th centuries. The oldest building is the Karuna Church, from 1686.

The next Scandinavian capital on our cruise was Stockholm, the largest city in Sweden, with a metropolitan population of more than two million. Stockholm is strategically located on 14 islands on the south-central east coast of Sweden at the mouth of Lake Mälaren.

Stockholm has a well-preserved and very interesting Old Town dating back to the Thirteenth Century and consisting of medieval alleyways, cobbled streets and archaic architecture. The Royal Palace, one of the largest in the world still used for its original purpose, is located in the Old Town area. This baroque structure was built in the Eighteenth Century after the previous palace burned down. Throughout the summer months, a formal changing-of-the-guard ceremony takes place early each afternoon. The marching guards and band made this a memorable experience.

Also while in Stockholm, we visited the Vasa Museum. The museum displays the 64-gun warship *Vasa* that foundered and sank in 1628 after sailing less than a nautical mile on her maiden voyage. Due to direct orders from the king to increase the ship's size after the construction had begun, the *Vasa* was built top-heavy and had insufficient ballast. Despite displaying an obvious lack of stability in port, she was allowed to set sail and foundered a few minutes later when she first encountered a wind stronger than a breeze.

Does it surprise you that orders from those who are in charge but who have little expertise can result in disaster?

Our final capital was Copenhagen, with a metropolitan population of 1.9 million. The highlight of our short stay there was a visit to the beautiful Rosenborg Castle, located in the city's center. The castle was originally built as a country summerhouse in 1606. It was constructed in the Dutch Renaissance style, typical of Danish buildings of this period, and has been expanded several times, finally evolving into its present condition by the year 1624.

Of special interest is a collection of porcelain, silverware and fine art, which have belonged to Danish monarchs through the ages. Situated in the King's Garden, the country's oldest royal garden, the castle also houses an impressive exhibition of the crown jewels and the Danish crown regalia.

We enjoyed our cruise of the Baltic Sea and the capitals of Scandinavia and would certainly recommend it to others. But whether you take a Baltic cruise or not, St. Petersburg is a MUST SEE. In fact, we spent a couple of days there again to begin our St. Petersburg to Moscow river cruise.

CHAPTER 37

RIVER CRUISES

If you like ocean cruising, you will love river cruising.
— Viking River Cruises

Thus far, my wife and I have taken three river cruises. The first was in Central Europe from Budapest to Amsterdam. The second trip was on the Yangtze River as part of our visit to China described in Chapter 39. Our most recent river cruise was on the lovely Doura River in Portugal. All three were great.

River cruises differ from ocean cruises in several ways. First, since there are no waves, so there is no chance of sea sickness. (Although, with computer-controlled undersea wing stabilizers, the chance of sea sickness on today's ocean cruises is very low.) Also, on our river cruises, most of the off-ship tours were preset by the cruise line, and the price of the tours was included in the cost of the trip up front.

River cruise ships are designed to pass through locks and are therefore very long and narrow (up to 450 feet long but only 37.5 feet wide). These sleek ships can accommodate from about 125 to 200 passengers. All cabins on a river cruise ship have an outside view; and although they are small, they are about the same size as cabins on much larger ocean cruise ships.

On our trips, dress has been very casual. Meals have also been casual, with no assigned seating. The food has been good and has often reflected local cuisine. Some folks got tired of the German sausages on our first cruise, but not me.

River cruising makes it very easy to meet and get to know your fellow passengers. With no assigned seating for meals, you are encouraged to share tables. Since everyone takes the same tours, you also have lots of contact with others during them. The best opportunity to get together is at the daily pre-dinner cocktail hour, where the cruise director conducts an informal briefing on the following day's itinerary. Another way to meet people is during the after-dinner activities. Some evenings feature local entertainment; others, a disc jockey for dancing or just enjoying the music over a nightcap.

For thousands of years, rivers have been the highway of commerce and trade. Cities, town and villages grew from the rivers inland. Therefore, most river communities have their centers on the river. From a ship docked in a city, it is usually a short walk to the main shopping and restaurant districts. Communities also line most rivers, so that travel from location to location usually doesn't take a lot of sailing time.

Because our first river cruise began in Budapest, Hungary, we decided to take a two-day pre-trip tour of the city. For us, Budapest was a very pleasant surprise. Budapest began as two cities and then merged. We stayed on the Buda side of the Danube River on a hill that provides a stunning view of the river, the lighted bridges and Pest across the way.

After leaving Budapest, the ship motored up the Danube to Bratislava, Slovakia. Bratislava is a very pretty old city. While we were there, it was full of young people enjoying the many outdoor eating and drinking establishments.

During our walking tour of Bratislava, we were shown a laser light system that at night was reflected from building to building. Starting from their City Hall, it lighted the main streets of the old city area. I was so intrigued by this laser light system that we walked back to the old city after dark to see it working.

When we arrived, the system was not working. After asking around for someone who spoke English and knew about the laser system, we learned that the laser had been "kaput" for several years. Moral of the story: don't always believe your tour guide.

The next day was really special. We docked at Vienna, one of Europe's most elegant and romantic cities. The day tour was spectacular. In addition, we attended an optional concert of compositions by Mozart and Strauss that evening at the Austrian Military History Museum.

One of the surprises of this trip for me was the visit to the dramatic 300-year-old baroque Melk Abbey located in Melk, Austria. This abbey, built from 1702 to 1736 and perched on sheer cliffs high above the Danube, has to be one of the most beautiful churches in the world.

The next three days included stops in Passau, Regemburg and Nuremberg, Germany. Passau has a wonderful gothic church. Regenburg is a well-preserved medieval city. Nuremberg was the location for the post-World War II war crimes trials and also includes the large parade grounds that were the site of many Nazi prewar rallies.

The next day was spent traversing the Main-Danube Canal. This engineering marvel stretches about 100 miles between the Danube and Main (pronounced: Mine) rivers. The canal was completed in 1992 and has 16 locks that raised the ship 1,332 feet.

As I recall, our ship went through a total of 67 locks during the 14 days of the cruise. Crossing through the locks was interesting the first few times. Especially impressive were the large vertical movements both up and down on the Main-Danube Canal locks. The ship crossed many of the locks at night while we slept and even a few times during days while we were off the ship touring.

The next few days included several more stops in German towns and villages as we sailed down the Main River. About this time in the cruise, our cruise director, a very cute German young lady named Annabel, explained that the schedule for the next several days would include "ABC." She explained that meant "another bloody church or cathedral," and of course she was correct.

At Mainz the Main River merges into the Rhine River, which we sailed for the rest of the trip. Our final large city stop was Cologne, where we visited the old city center and the beautiful Cathedral of Cologne. It took 700 years to complete this huge structure, which was one of only a few building in Cologne not damaged by Allied bombing during World War II.

We disembarked at Amsterdam. This is a very unusual city with canals, interesting sights and terrific museums. An evening stroll through the famous Amsterdam red-light district is also a must.

In addition to the many shore excursions on the trip, there were a few times when the ship would sail from one town to the next during part of the day. This gave us the opportunity to spend leisurely hours on the large deck on the top of the ship just watching the landscape go by. One stretch was particularity scenic as we cruised past several old castles on the cliffs beside of the river.

This is another big difference between river and ocean cruising. On the river you are always close to both shores and can even interact with the people on the banks. This was one of our favorite parts of river cruising.

Our most recent river cruise was in the second half of September, grape harvest time, on the Doura River in Portugal. A travel agent whom we met and befriended on the Central European river cruise put together a special group of compatible people, which made this especially enjoyable.

The tour part of this trip started in Lisbon, the capital of Portugal and also the country's largest city, with a population of about three million people. Lisbon is a very old city dating back to 1200 B.C.

We spent three nights enjoying the city and the areas around Lisbon. Our tours included the old Alfama district, built originally by the Moors when they inhabited this part of Portugal. Another highlight was the National Coach Museum. We also visited a beautiful coffee shop where we were told J. K. Rowling had begun to write the blockbuster Harry Potter books. I later found that the coffee shop in question was actually in Porto, Portugal.

The next day was spent busing from Lisbon north to Porto at the mouth of the Doura River. At Porto we boarded the ship for the evening. The next day we toured this charming medieval city on a steep hill on the north river bank.

For the next six days we sailed up the Doura River to the Spanish border at Vega de Terron and back to Porto. The Doura is not wide, and its valley is narrow with steep hills on both sides. As we left Porto, these hillsides were covered with grape vineyards. A little further upstream we passed through areas of almond trees and then olive trees, but the main crop by far was grapes.

During our trip, up the river and back down, we stopped at five Portuguese towns or villages. We toured wineries, had several chances to taste various port wines and had a wonderful dinner off the ship at the former Fourteenth Century Benedictine Monastery of Alpendurada.

We also spent one day visiting Salamanca, Spain. Salamanca is known both for its monumental sights and for the University of Salamanca. Founded in 1218 the university is the oldest in Spain and the fifth oldest university in the western world. Christopher Columbus once lectured here on his discoveries in what he and his financial backers thought were the Indies.

A main attraction for any visitor to Salamanca is the Plaza Mayor, the central square, regarded as one of the finest in Europe. Originally built for bullfights, the plaza can hold 20,000 people for concerts and is surrounded by shaded arcades full of shops and restaurants. Other main attractions include an old Romanesque cathedral, which was founded in the Twelfth Century, and the adjoining "new" cathedral which was constructed in stages beginning in 1509 and was still being finished in 1734.

Our tour was taken during harvest time for the Toruiga Francesa grapes used to make the world famous *vinho do porto*, or port wine. Port is a sweet red wine which is often served as a desert wine. I love it after dinner with cheese.

Port is the Portuguese version of fortified wine. Port is fortified by adding a neutral grape spirit to stop the fermentation process early, leaving residual sugar. Fortifying the wine also increases the alcohol content.

Since it was harvest time, we often exchanged shouted greetings with the grape harvesters working the vineyards on the hillsides as we sailed up and down the Doura. We were also fortunate to be in one of the small towns for their evening harvest festival parade and fireworks over the river.

As I hope you can see, river cruising is a great way to tour. We have enjoyed each of our three river cruises so much that in 2010 we took one from St. Petersburg to Moscow in July and a Nile River cruise in Egypt in October.

CHAPTER 38

LAND-BASED TOURS

Wherever you go, there you are.
— *Carl Franz, author of The People's Guide to Mexico*

Land-based tours can either involve lots of suit-case packing, lots of bus or airplane time, or both. This doesn't necessarily mean that these tours should be avoided, since this is the only way to get to some locations. It does mean that you need to understand what you're getting into when you sign up.

You can either book one of the many land-based tours organized by travel outfitters or set up a tour yourself, as my golf group often did. A few years ago, my wife and I spent two weeks touring Italy with four other couples.

One of the couples in our group had lived and worked for a couple of years in Zurich, Switzerland. This couple planned our trip, so we started by flying to Zurich. There we rented two nine-passenger vans, primarily for the luggage that our spouses brought along. We started our trip by spending two days seeing the city of Zurich and the beautiful surrounding area. While in the area, we even visited a small local cheese factory.

Our first destination in Italy was a rented villa on Lake Cuomo. Getting from Zurich to Lake Cuomo normally involves driving through a major tunnel under the Alps. However, a day or two before our trip, a landslide closed the road to the tunnel, so we had to take the old route over a high pass. This added several hours to the trip, but the scenery almost made it worthwhile.

The villa we rented was a large three-story house built in the 1300s and updated in about the 1700s. The accommodations didn't meet the expectations of the female members of our group, but the location on the bank of Lake Cuomo and the large shaded yard made up for the minor inconveniences found inside. At least it did for me. Our deal for the villa included a chef for two dinners, which were outstanding.

Lake Cuomo is widely and justifiably regarded as one of the most beautiful lakes in the world. Our villa was on the west side of the lake near the town of Menaggio and very close to the world class Villa d'Este hotel. We were only a couple of miles north of George Clooney's vacation home. Our wives shouted to George from both the lake and the road without any response. He must not have been in residence during our visit, or surely he would have come outside.

While in the area we took a day trip to Lugano, Switzerland, and visited the small town of Bellagio on the east side of Lake Cuomo. We also enjoyed visiting Villa del Balbianello, famous for its elaborate terraced gardens. It was built in 1787 on the site of a Franciscan monastery and recently was the final home of the adventurer and mountain climber Guido Monzino. Today, the villa houses an interesting museum devoted to his many feats and travels.

We also took a train trip from the city of Cuomo to Venice, changing trains in Milan. Train travel in Europe is very convenient and reasonably priced, and the trains run on time. Venice was as wonderful as I'd expected. Some say that it is expensive (it is); others say that it smells bad (if it did, I didn't notice it); but in any case, Venice is a MUST for any traveler. Venice is a small city packed into a very small area. The population of the city itself is only about 270,000, although the metropolitan area has a population of 1.6 million.

Venice is built on 118 little islands. Moving around requires walking across bridges over the many canals, using water buses, taking one of the many water taxis or relaxing in a romantic Venetian gondola.

The center of Venice is the Piazza San Marco, or St. Mark's Square, a large open area laid out in 1199 on the bank of the Grand Canal. The buildings around the square are fabulous. The most important is the Doge's Palace. From this large building, built between 1309 and 1424, the rulers of Venice (the doges) ruled the western world well into the 1500's. Venice was not governed by politicians, as such, but by the most financially successful businessmen in the city. The large group would elect a much smaller group as a type of executive committee. The small group would then elect one from their group to be the doge and act as their head. As a check and balance in their system, the doge could say "no" to the remaining group but could not overrule a "no" from them.

At one time a doge suggested that he should be named king so that he could make all the decisions unilaterally. After a short time to consider this suggestion, the rest of group had him arrested and hanged. Not such a bad system, perhaps.

As you would expect for the building that housed the rulers of the western world, the Doge's Palace is magnificently decorated. The building also holds the court. Attached to the palace, across the "Bridge of Sighs" over one of the many small canals, is the prison. Touring the palace and the prison is a must.

Also on St. Mark's Square are St. Mark's Basilica, many shops and restaurants in the large covered arcade, and a tall, free-standing bell tower. The bell tower, or campanile, was built in 1912 to replace the one completed in 1514 that collapsed in 1902. The campanile is very impressive at 36 feet by 36 feet and 323 feet tall. You can actually walk to the top for a great view. I passed.

After spending seven days on Lake Cuomo, our small group drove south to our next villa located just outside of the city of Lucca in Tuscany. Situated on the central west coast of Italy north of Rome, Tuscany is one of the 20 regions of Italy.

Lucca is famous for its intact Renaissance-era city walls. The city was founded by the Etruscans and became a Roman colony in 180 B.C. The rectangular grid of its historical center preserves the Roman street plan, and the Piazza San Michele occupies the site of the ancient forum. The Piazza San Michele is in front of the San Michele in Foro Church, which has an unusual facade of many different ornate columns.

Traces of Lucca's original Roman amphitheatre can still be seen in the oblong Piazza dell'Anfiteatro. The old city of Lucca is filled with many interesting restaurants and shops, including a wonderful wine shop with a very impressive wine cellar. Our villa's owner had arranged with this shop for a wonderful afternoon of wine-tasting at the villa. As with Lake Cuomo, our Lucca villa came with a chef and some great in-villa meals.

Lucca is a reasonably central home base from which to explore Tuscany by car. The capital of the region is Florence, the home of some of the world's most famous art and loveliest architecture. No trip to Tuscany can be complete without seeing this fabled city. However, even if you have rented a car, the best way to travel from Lucca to Florence is by train, because of the difficulty of parking in Florence.

In Florence, a local guide is essential to get you past the long lines for almost all of the key venues. To me, the most impressive sight was Michelangelo's large statue of David, located in the Galleria dell Accademia.

Another very interesting excursion from Lucca is a day trip to Cinque Terre, which lies north and west along the Mediterranean coast and which I described in Chapter 34 on Mediterranean cruises

A third rewarding day trip is to Siena, south of Florence. The city's best-known feature is the large, shell-shaped Piazza del Campo, the town square, famous for hosting the Palio horse race.

The Palio di Siena is a traditional medieval horse race between the various neighborhoods in the city run around the Piazza del Campo twice each year, on July 2 and August 16. The event is attended by huge crowds and is widely televised. In fact, this race made an impression on me early in my life. I can remember watching the race on "Wide World of Sports" on black and white television and dreaming that someday I might see that beautiful square. And I did!

Not far from Siena is the wonderful walled small medieval village of San Gimignano, which is built on a hill overlooking the picturesque Tuscan landscape. This village is famous for its medieval architecture, especially its towers, which can be seen from several kilometers outside the town.

In medieval times in this part of Italy, many families or groups built tall, thin towers where they would stay when enemies attacked the town. In other cities, such as Bologna or Florence, most or all of the towers have been brought down due to wars, catastrophes, or urban renewal. San Gimignano has managed to conserve 14 towers of varying height, and these have become its international symbol.

Shopping was good in San Gimignano. We bought some Italian pottery and even purchased a large original oil painting of the Tuscan countryside, which hangs prominently in our home.

Lucca is close to Pisa. A quick trip to see the leaning tower, which leans more that I would have thought, and take a picture of someone holding up the tower is about all you need to do there.

A week in Tuscany with friends is well worth the time and money. On this trip, we did a lot of driving (I was one of the two van drivers) but were on our own schedule, saw a lot of the countryside and had a truly great time.

Our two most recent land-based tours were organized by travel professionals. The first of these followed the Doura River cruise described in Chapter 37. After we left our ship in Porto, Portugal, we flew with a small group to Madrid, the capital of Spain and a very large metropolitan area, with a population of almost six million people. During this tour, we spent all four nights in Madrid.

The first day, we toured around Madrid and visited the Prado Museum. The Prado features one of the world's finest collections of European art, from the Twelfth Century to the early Nineteenth, and has easily the world's finest collection of Spanish painting, including large numbers of the finest works of Diego Velázquez, Francisco Goya and El Greco.

Our next excursion was a day trip via high speed train to Seville, a city of about 1.5 million people southwest of Madrid. While our time in Seville was short, it was well worth the effort.

Most impressive was our visit to the Cathedral of Seville, which was built between 1401 and 1519 on the former site of the city's mosque. It ranks among the largest of all medieval gothic cathedrals, in terms of both area and volume. The interior is lavishly decorated with a huge quantity of gold evident, especially on the retable or altarpiece behind the main chapel.

In Seville, we also visited the House of Pilate, so-called because it was thought to resemble the residence of Pontius Pilate in Jerusalem. After traveling in the Holy Land and in Italy, where he became enamored of Renaissance architecture, the first Marquis of Tarifa built this beautiful palace in the early 1500s. It is a large building covered with thousands of ceramic tiles of many different designs in the Moorish style. Still occupied, now by the Dukes of Medinaceli, this house was recently featured in the 2010 movie "Knight and Day" staring Tom Cruise and Cameron Diaz.

No trip to Seville would be complete without a carriage ride through Maria Luisa Park and the Avenue of the Delights with a stop at the unbelievable Plaza de Espana, one of Seville's most easily recognized landmarks. Erected to host the 1929 Spanish-American Exhibition and accessible over a moat by numerous beautiful bridges, the plaza is a huge half-circle with buildings running continually around the edge. There is a large fountain in the center of the decorative brick plaza. All parts of the buildings, bridges and railings are covered with colorful ceramic tiles.

As impressive as both Madrid and Seville were, nothing prepared us for the highlight of our brief stay in Spain. Toledo is the country's real jewel. A small city with a population of only 80,000, Toledo is located only about 45 miles from Madrid, so our day trip was made on a mini bus. For many years, Toledo was the center of religion in that part of the world, with large groups of Christians, Muslims and Jews practicing their faiths in harmony. Some believe that this focus on religion was the origin of the popular exclamation "Holy Toledo!"

The medieval wall around the old city is still intact in many places. Toledo was also protected by the high and steep banks of the River Tajo, which flanks the city on the east, south and west. The old city is wonderful, but the best of the best is the cathedral and its sacristy full of magnificent works of art.

The cathedral of Toledo was begun in 1226 and completed in 1493. It is ranked among the greatest Gothic structures in Europe. Its beautiful retable contains more than a dozen colorfully painted scenes from the Bible. The cathedral receives its light through more than 750 stained glass windows, dating from the Fourteenth, Fifteenth and Sixteenth Centuries, the work of some of the best artists of those times.

Directly behind the main altar is El Transparente, which stands out among the cathedral's many art treasures. A wall of marble and florid baroque alabaster sculpture, it was overlooked for years because the cathedral was too poorly lit. Starting in 1721 and ending in 1732, sculptor Narcisco Tomé cut a skylight in the ceiling to allow sunlight to reach the high-rising angels, a Last Supper in alabaster and a Virgin in ascension. This hidden hole in the roof results in a truly an amazing effect.

But again, the best was left until last. Located off the left side of the sanctuary is the sacristy. This moderately-sized room contains some of the best and most valuable art in the world. The ceiling is wonderfully painted, but the paintings hanging in the room are truly incredible. They include Goya's famous "Arrest of Christ on the Mount of Olives" and El Greco's "Twelve Apostles" and "Spoliation of Christ." There are 14 other paintings by El Greco and a number by other important European artists. Anyone who visits the great sights of Europe gets to see many large and beautiful cathedrals, as my wife and I have, but none has been as wonderful as the Cathedral of Toledo.

Our most recent land-based tour took us to Italy's Amalfi Coast, renowned for its scenic grandeur, rugged terrain, amazing vertical landscape, picturesque towns, narrow twisting roads and varied architecture. This trip was booked through a university alumni association.

For this trip we flew into Naples and bused south over a rugged mountain range to a hotel above the town of Amalfi. Amalfi was founded by the Romans in the Fourth Century A.D. This small seaside resort enjoys an ideal climate and offers breathtaking views of the Mediterranean Sea. The most impressive monument in Amalfi is the cathedral, with its unusual two-colored façade. The cathedral was founded prior to the Ninth Century. Amalfi's main square in front of the cathedral and the main street that runs up the hill away from the harbor are lined with interesting shops and restaurants. This is a tourist's town.

Using our hotel above Amalfi as a base, for the next seven days we took bus trips to visit other towns in the area. Most of this travel was along the narrow, winding, steep and sometimes scary Amalfi Coast road. This two-lane road runs 28 miles along the Gulf of Solerno from Sorrento on the west to Salerno on the east. Amalfi is located roughly in the center. This road has many switchbacks as it winds up and down along the steep cliffs. In many places only one bus or truck can enter the switchback at a time. In a few places, a bus or truck has to enter the switchback and then back up to complete the turn. The road is very busy with buses, lots of small cars, motorcycles and big trucks, so travel on it is very slow.

The views of the water and the landscape are magnificent, but driving is very difficult. To make the trips even more interesting, our group was traveling in a medium large bus. During our time in the area, our bus with a very experienced driver brushed the concrete guard rail twice and was sideswiped by one car. I would not recommend renting a car and driving in this area.

Early in our tour, we visited the small village of Revello and the town of Sorrento. In Revello, we toured the beautiful Villa Rufolo, which had a wonderful view of the coast. Sorrento was a very long bus ride each way, so on this trip we didn't have time to see much beyond the main square and the town's shopping streets.

Next we traveled from Amalfi via boat to the lovely seaside resort of Positano, known as Italy's most vertical town. Positano has charming pastel-colored houses that cluster along magnificent terraces and narrow lanes lined with elegant boutiques, lively bars, restaurants and cafes.

One of the best days of our Amalfi Coast tour was a visit to the preserved ruins of Herculaneum and Pompeii. These two villages were destroyed and preserved by being covered by ash from a violent eruption of the volcano Vesuvius in the year 79 A.D. I had always heard about Pompeii and was not disappointed. But Herculaneum for me was even better. While the site is not nearly as large as Pompeii, the condition and size of the buildings, especially the central baths, was very interesting. When you visit Pompeii, do not miss Herculaneum.

Our next visit was to the Isle of Capri again from Amalfi via boat. Capri has been described previously in Chapter 34. We have now visited Capri three times, and I am sure we will visit this lovely place again. It is special.

The last two destinations of our tour were Paestum and Salerno to the east of Amalfi. Paestum is the home to two of the best-preserved Greek temples north of Sicily. The older, the Temple of Hera, was built by Greek colonists around 550 B.C. Located nearby is the second temple of Hera. Built around 450 B.C., it is about 200 feet long, and all of the structure survives except the roof and the internal walls. Both temples are well worth seeing.

We had an unusual but interesting day in Salerno. We visited a buffalo mozzarella cheese farm and factory. Buffalo mozzarella is made from water buffalo milk. The farm was totally integrated and organic. They grew their buffalo feed; they raised, bred and milked the water buffalo cows; and they processed the buffalo milk into cheese. It was easy for them to use organic fertilizer to grow the feed, because of the large amount of buffalo droppings available to them. (This is in here for those of you who do not have a good understanding of what "organic" really means.)

Most interesting to me was the automatic milking of the cows. When the cows were nearly ready to be milked, they were moved into a nice shed with feed troughs and rubbers mats for them to lie on. When they decided that they wanted to be milked, they would enter an area with two large self-starting wheel brushes with long bristles, where they would get scratched and cleaned. The cows seemed to really enjoy this "spa" treatment.

Next the cows would stand in a line until the milking robot was available. When it was her turn, the next cow would enter the milking area, her udder would be sprayed with a cleaning solution, and the milking devices would be automatically attached to each of her teats. We were told that each cow had an imbedded chip that told the robot who she was so that the machine would know the locations of each of her teats. After the milking, the raw milk was pumped to the cheese factory where the mozzarella was made and finished by hand. I have to say there is no cheese as good as fresh warm mozzarella just out of the factory.

While our land tour was a good way to see the entire Amalfi region, and taking day trips from our hotel allowed us to avoid the hassles of packing and unpacking every couple of days, this mode of travel did involve a lot of time on the bus. You can also visit the area by cruise ship, but you do miss experiencing the torturous but scenic Amalfi Coast road.

With land tours, like any other type of travel, planning well and setting realistic expectations will make the trip much more enjoyable.

CHAPTER 39

CHINA

A journey of a thousand miles begins with a single step.
— Lao-tzu, Chinese philosopher (c. 600 B.C.)

There are many things that have to be seen to be believed. The Great Wall of China is certainly one of them. Some astronauts have even claimed to be able to see it with their naked eyes from orbit. Erected by a succession of emperors as a defense against the marauding nomadic tribes of the north, the Great Wall extends 4,000 miles from east to west in northern China. It took almost 2,000 years to build over some of the roughest mountain terrain that I have ever seen.

The Great Wall is not the only reason to visit China, but it is certainly a highlight of the trip. When we visited the Great Wall, we could only actually see a couple of miles of the wall and only walked along it maybe a mile; but with that limited view, we could begin to imagine the magnitude of the entire construction. Not only is it long, but it is high and wide; and where we visited outside Beijing, it was also steep.

Our trip to China began with three days in the capital, Beijing. Beijing is a very large city with a population of over 13 million residents. The first thing we noticed was the number of new large buildings being constructed. There must have been 50 or more buildings of 40 stories or more under way. We were there the year before the Olympic Summer Games, and it was very busy. We also visited Tiananmen Square (the largest public square in the world) during the week when the Chinese were celebrating the victory of 1953. Red and yellow flowers were everywhere around the city, but Tiananmen Square had the largest display. Because it was a holiday week, the square was filled with people. This is where I observed more than 100 men using about 40 urinals, two or three men at each urinal at the same time. Also in Beijing we visited the Forbidden City, the emperor's summer palace and the Beijing Opera.

Next we flew to Xi'an, one of China's many multimillion population cities that is unknown to most westerners. Located in central China, Xi'an is a city of more than eight million people. The prime reason for visiting Xi'an is to see the Terra Cotta Warriors. Over 2,000 years ago, Emperor Qin Shi Huangdi had thousands of life-sized warriors and horses made from terra cotta (fired clay) to guard the site of his tomb. This site was only discovered in 1974 (by a local farmer) and is still being excavated.

From Xi'an we flew to Chongqing, a city of five million and the capital of a region with a population of over 30 million. Chongqing was our embarkation point for a three-day cruise of the Yangtze River. Our cruise included some stops along the river, but the highlight was cruising through the Qutang Gorge with its high peaks and sheer cliffs. This stretch of the river is often depicted in Chinese paintings.

The cruise ended at Yichang, where we were able to tour the tremendous Three Gorges Dam. By any measure the project is massive. The dam itself is over 1.4 miles long and contains 32 massive electricity generators. We were told that the project was estimated to cost about $25 billion, which included $10 billion to relocate 1.3 million people whose homes would be flooded by the resulting reservoir.

According to what we were told, the Three Gorges Dam is actually the second in a series of 20 or so dams planned for the Yangtze River over the next 40 years. This is really long-term planning. When I heard this, I had to lament that the U.S. cannot even get an energy policy approved.

From Yichang we flew to Shanghai, the largest city in China. This truly amazing metropolis of more than 20 million people is located on the Yangtze River downstream from the Three Gorges Dam. The architecture near the river is a mixture of early Twentieth Century western European buildings and skyscrapers so modern they could serve as backdrops for a science fiction film. One highlight of our brief stay in Shanghai was spending an evening at a performance of the Acrobats of Shanghai.

Next, the group flew to Hong Kong. This great city has seven million people living in a very small area. Western hotels and shopping areas abound.

A highlight for us in Hong Kong was the nightly multicolored neon light show on the buildings in the main business area on Hong Kong Island. We stayed across Victoria Harbor on the Kowloon side, which gave us a spectacular view of the show.

Another highlight was a day trip to the Hong Kong Zoo, which is actually a combination zoo and amusement park. The zoo is built on a very hilly island, but a sky lift moves visitors through the attractions. For us, the best of these was the panda exhibit. At the time we were there, they had a pair of two-year-old panda twins and about five adults. It is a rare and special treat to see these endangered animals in person.

By now, you probably have reached the conclusion that I was very impressed by what we saw in China. You are certainly correct. On the down side, due to pollution we didn't see the sun for two weeks, even though the weather was good.

Travel to and inside China is easy. (Of course, it is a long flight there and back.) The hotels are equal to good American hotels. The Chinese food is like the dishes you would find in any Chinese restaurant in the U.S., only better. In the bigger cities (and almost all Chinese cities are "bigger cities") you will encounter McDonald's, Friday's, Starbucks and even Pizza Hut, in case you want a taste of home.

The Chinese people are friendly and love to practice speaking English. The only area of concern can be finding a western toilet in some of the remote stops along the way.

If by now you have committed to developing a "bucket list," I would recommend putting China near the top.

CHAPTER 40

SAFARIS

There is always something new out of Africa.
— Pliny the Elder (23-79 A.D.)

One of the best trips my wife and I have ever taken was a safari to southern Africa. Dictionary. com defines "safari" as "a journey or expedition, for hunting, exploration, or investigation." Ours didn't involve hunting, but it certainly involved the other two features.

Sue Ann and I both love animals. All types of animals. In fact, she has just interrupted my writing to have me admire an osprey eating a fish in a pine tree in our backyard. (I don't think of fish as animals.)

Because of our love of animals, we joined the Columbus Zoo years ago. We enjoyed taking the kids to the zoo, and we also enjoyed the annual members' party. During our years at the zoo, we became friends with its director, Jerry Borin, and his wife, Lois. A couple of times a year, Jerry, who has since retired, had the enviable job of leading tours to Africa and other exotic places so that the participants could see and learn about the animals in the wild. A portion of the price of these tours benefited the zoo's coffers.

In one of my conversations with Jerry, I mentioned my interest in visiting Africa and my willingness to put together a group of friends to make the trip. A few months later, he called and said that he'd arranged a photo safari. All I needed to do was enlist six other couples, which with Jerry and Lois and me and Sue Ann would make 16 people total.

I was able to pull together a potential group quickly, but they were skeptical about the accommodations. The biggest challenge for Jerry and Lois was convincing the suburban housewives, and a couple of their husbands, most of whom had never been camping, that sleeping in canvas tents in the wilds of Africa was no big deal. Jerry and Lois were even able to persuade my wife that these fully-staffed camps would have a lot in common with a Ritz-Carlton.

The trip would begin with a nonstop but very long flight from Atlanta to Johannesburg, South Africa. After recuperating for a night in a fine hotel, we would take a commercial flight to Mann, Botswana. From Mann, we were to take two single-engine planes to our first camp. After two nights there, we would go on to a second camp and then a third. Next we would fly to Victoria Falls, Zimbawe, also for two nights, then take a commercial flight to Cape Town, South Africa, for a final three days of sightseeing.

Because we'd be flying on those small single-engine planes, each person was allowed to bring only 26 pounds of stuff in duffle bags for the entire two-week trip. We were told that the camp staff would gladly wash all of our clothing, except for "smalls," the British term for underwear. This luggage limitation presented my first problem. My wife routinely travels with 30 pounds of cosmetics and electrical devices; so we split our 52 pound allowance. I got to take 15 pounds, and she took the rest.

The flight to Johannesburg was long but well worth the discomfort. After a night's rest and the commercial flight to Botswana, we boarded one of the single-engine planes for the short hop to the first camp, in the Okavango Delta region.

The Okavango River floods every spring creating many large islands. The plentiful water attracts huge numbers of animals to this area. This isn't a jungle, like where Tarzan and Jane lived, but a dry, flat plane with vast open areas and punctuated by scrub brush and small trees. We were there in June and early July, which is the dry season. The weather was wonderful, with nighttime temperatures in the low 60s, daytime highs near 90 with very little humidity and not a cloud in the sky.

Each of our three camps consisted of a main building, where we took meals and relaxed, and eight to ten guest tents, plus separate structures for the camp employees. The tents had permanent wood bases with canvas tops. Each contained a double bed and an indoor toilet and shower. Some of the camps also had outdoor showers for each tent.

Because the tents were unheated, they were cold at night. At one camp, I quickly undressed and jumped into bed, only to have my feet hit something hot under the covers. According to my wife, I screamed like a teenaged girl as I jumped out of bed. Throwing back the covers, I found a hot water bottle, which, after my heart rate returned to normal, I grew to enjoy.

A day at the camps started with a wake-up drum. We weren't allowed to venture out of the tents on our own, since the camps were unfenced and we could encounter wild animals. After the grounds were closely checked, a member of the staff would visit each tent and escort the occupants to the main building for coffee and a light breakfast.

Next came the morning animal drive. We headed out in open Land Rovers, each with a driver and a guide but no guns. On top behind the driver and guide were three stair-stepped elevated bench seats, giving us a breathtaking 360-degree view of the animals. This drive lasted about two hours, with a break on the plain for coffee and snacks. During this break, the Midwestern housewives learned to use the "bush toilet." After a little practice squatting, most did well, although occasionally one would end up with a yellow sock.

The animal drive was followed by an excellent full-course breakfast, then three or four hours to rest and clean up. After lunch, we were treated to a late afternoon animal drive and a "sun setter" on the plain. The vehicles would meet at a designated location, where the camp employees had set up a bar with hors d'oeuvres. There is nothing like seeing the sun set across the African plain while viewing the animals in the foreground!

To celebrate our Independence Day, on the Fourth of July the staff prepared a special sun setter with hot dogs and popcorn.

The plains and the animals look different and much scarier at night. After our sun setter, the guides would take us on a short animal tracking, using footprints and droppings to identify and follow the big cats and other species and pointing them out with spotlights. The areas around our camps were so full of animals that they were easy to spot.

During the daily animal drives, we saw large groups of zebra mixed with giraffe, antelope and wildebeest. Warthogs were everywhere. (Because the tail of the warthog sticks straight up, the guides referred to them as "radio Botswana.") Hyenas were plentiful, as were vultures to clean up the kills of others. Elephants roamed freely, indifferent to us and to the rest of the animals.

The most amazing animals were the great cats. Leopards were scarce and hard to spot; they kept their distance. Cheetahs were also shy, but we saw them every day. But the King of the Jungle, and I'm sure the plains also, is the lion. They totally ignored the vehicles and continued to eat their kills, even when a Land Rover came within 20 or 30 feet of their feast. They were bigger than I'd expected them to be, and their roar, especially at night when you're in your tent, can keep you awake. At least it did me.

The employees at all the camps were wonderful people who spoke reasonable English and wanted to practice their English and learn about us. On our last night at each camp, they put on a singing and dancing show to wish us on our way. Our group decided to reciprocate by teaching the staff at each camp some simple magic tricks and the song that starts: "If you're happy and you know it, clap your hands."

To begin, a friend and I did the trick called "Black Magic." This is a simple routine in which someone, in this case me, leaves the area, and an object is selected for later identification. After saying "no" to several items, I identified the correct item, only to have a woman employee shriek and faint. After that demonstration, I received especially good treatment from the camp employees for the rest of my time at that camp.

By the third camp, our fame had preceded us. The employees wanted to see our acts the first night, so that they could learn the tricks and the song.

Although Sue Ann and I have had many good trips, this safari was the best so far. On this trip, it all came together. The location, the weather, the accommodations, the scenery and the animals were all outstanding. So were the people – the staffs of the camps, our traveling companions and especially Lois and Jerry Borin, who set it all up and answered our many questions before and during the trip.

In the first chapter of this section, I recommended that you make a "bucket list" of places to visit and things to do. No bucket list would be complete without a visit to Africa to see the animals in their natural habitat. A safari was even on the list in the movie.

We took our safari before my retirement, and I recommend that you put yours early on your list, because even the cushiest safari does require a certain amount of mobility and stamina.

CHAPTER 41

HAWAII: THE JOY OF STAYING PUT

There is no place in the world like Hawaii.
— Hawaii Visitors and Convention Bureau

The Hawaii Visitors and Convention Bureau certainly has it right: there is no place in the world like Hawaii. We love it.

Hawaii was formed millions of years ago by a series of volcanic eruptions that started from a single magma source at the bottom of the sea about 14,000 feet below the surface. The movement of the tectonic plate shifted the earth's crust over this hot spot to the southeast over millions of years, with the result that the islands migrated to the northwest. The most westerly island, Kauai, is estimated to be more than five million years old, while the most easterly island, the Big Island or the Island of Hawaii, rose out of the ocean only about 400,000 years ago.

When they were formed, Hawaii's volcanic mountains were extremely steep. However, over the millions of years, the mountains on the most westerly islands have been worn down by the rains and wind. The most easterly island, the Big Island, still has an active volcano that has been erupting since 1983.

My wife and I started visiting Hawaii in the early 1990s and have returned about 15 times. Our first trip was to the island of Kauai, where I had won a fully-paid one-week stay at Poipu Beach on the south coast in a charity golf tournament.

When we landed in Honolulu to catch a local flight to Kauai, we could not find Kauai listed as a destination on the airline flight screen. When we asked, we were told that the flight was actually to Lihue, the town where Kauai's airport is located. This is common in Hawaii. You not only need to know the island where you are going but also the city with the airport.

Kauai is called the Garden Island. Like all of Hawaii's islands, it is lush and green, especially on the northwest, windward, side. On Kauai, the northwest coast is called the Na Pali coast. Here the green valleys are separated by steep cliffs, making them accessible only from the sea. A boat ride along this coast is very worthwhile.

Over the years, the Na Pali coast has served as a location for several movies, including "South Pacific" (1958) and more recently "Jurassic Park."

Also on Kauai, we hiked to the "wettest spot on earth" in the low mountains not far from Poipu, and took a helicopter ride through spectacular Waimea Canyon, which is called the "Grand Canyon of the Pacific." The helicopter ride is well worth the time and money.

Some people call the helicopter the state bird of Hawaii, because these aerial sightseeing trips are so popular with tourists. Helicopters are a great way to see and enjoy the many incredibly beautiful parts of the islands that are otherwise inaccessible.

During this trip to Kauai, I played golf at the Kauai Lagoons Kiele course, which is laid out beside the ocean and offers spectacular views. I've heard good things about the golf courses at Princeville, on the north coast, but I've yet to play any of them.

On our second trip to Hawaii, we took our two children to Maui. Called the Valley Island, Maui is the second largest of the Hawaiian islands. It was formed from the combination of two large volcanoes. As the tectonic plate moved, lava flowed from the newer of the two volcanoes, Haleakala, or "House of the Sun," to fill the void between the two about one million years ago.

In my estimation, Maui is the best of the islands for a family vacation. There are more resorts, more beaches and more activities. The best snorkeling in Hawaii is at the Molokini Crater, an ancient volcanic caldera submerged near the surface two miles off South Maui.

This was our first encounter with the wonderful humpback whales. Each year from November through May about 10,000 humpback whales journey 4,000 miles from their Alaska feeding grounds to Hawaii to give birth and breed. These air-breathing mammals can reach 45 feet in length and weigh up to 90,000 pounds. It is thrilling to see their 20-foot spout; hear their "blow," which can be audible for up to 800 feet; and smell the extremely fishy odor of their exhalations when they come to the surface to breath. An even bigger thrill is to see them breach or jump almost all the way out of the water only to make a huge splash on re-entry.

No trip to Hawaii is complete without at least one whale-watching cruise. The best is a sunset whale-watch with drinks!

The airport on Maui is at Kahului on the north side of the saddle between the volcanoes, but the town of Lahaina is Maui's tourism hub. From 1843 until 1860, it was the center of whaling activity in the islands. Today it has a Whaling Museum, lots of shops and good restaurants. Many of Maui's large hotels lie along the beach next to Lahaina.

No one should visit Maui without driving to the top of the larger of the two volcanoes, which is protected as a national park. If you're feeling intrepid, are wearing sturdy footwear (NOT beach sandals) and have packed some water, you can hike down into the crater. (You can even make reservations ahead of time to camp in primitive cabins on the crater floor.) But if a day-long hike sounds like too much work, you can opt instead for the awe-inspiring view from the overlook. On a clear day from the top of Haleakala, at 10,023 feet, you can see the Big Island about 90 miles to the southeast. I have been told that seeing the sun rise from the top is magnificent. This happened way too early for my family.

I have played golf on Maui. There are great courses at the Kapalua resort on the west coast, at

Kaanapali resort area just south of Kapalua also on the west coast, and at Wailea on the south coast.

Our next island to discover was Hawaii, or the Big Island, which quickly became our favorite. This island was formed by two volcanoes that are now extinct and a new volcano that is still erupting and still growing the island. The two extinct volcanoes are both spectacular. The oldest is Mauna Kea. At its summit at 13,796 feet, a consortium of universities has installed 12 very large telescopes studying the universe. The comparative lack of light pollution and the position of Hawaii in the middle of the Pacific, allowing astronomers there to search the skies at different times from their colleagues on the mainland, make it one of the world's most important observatories.

A guided trip up Mauna Kea for sunset and stargazing is well worth it. It will be cold (there is snow on top and even some adventuresome skiers during the winter months); but the tour operators carry warm jackets, gloves and hot soup.

When you land on the west side of the Big Island, the resort side, you land at the Kailua-Kona airport. The town of Kailua and most activities are about 20 minutes south of the airport. Our favorite place is the Mauna Lani resort about 30 minutes north of the airport on the Kohala Coast.

The drive north from the airport is a little like driving on the moon. The road is cut through a series of lava flows that have spilled out of the volcano Mauna Loa (13,677 feet) over the past few hundred years. The scenery is spectacular, with the very high volcanoes on your right and the beautiful deep blue Pacific Ocean on your left.

The Big Island offers lots of things to do. Our favorite was to show the entire island to visiting friends or family. We would start by driving north to the quaint village of Hawi to see a statue of King Kamehameha the Great, the leader who unified the islands in 1810 and preserved their independence by negotiating alliances with major colonial powers. We would also visit some of Hawi's small stores and the community center. Driving south to Waimea, we would cross cattle country, sometimes passing *paniolas*, Hawaiian cowboys, on horseback. Then we would drive across the north coast, stopping to see valley overlooks and waterfalls. Next, on to Hilo, the commercial center of the island (and the location of the second airport), for lunch.

Continuing south we would reach Volcano National Park, which sits on the active volcano Kilauea. Here a visit to the information center and a drive around the Kilauea Crater are very interesting. The final leg of our tour would take us around the south side of the island to Kailua for dinner. This trip takes a full day but is well worth it.

A helicopter flight over the active Kilauea Volcano and the beautiful Waipio Valley on the north coast is a must to complete any visit to the Big Island.

There are lots of golf courses on the Big Island, I have played most of them. My favorites are a Kea, Hualalai, Mauna Lani south, Hapuna Kona Country Club Alii mountain course.

Most flights to and from Hawaii go through the Honolulu airport on the island of Oahu. One of the most famous beaches in the world is Waikiki. You may want to stop and take a look, but don't bother to change into your swimsuit. The beach is rocks, not sand, and is only one block from downtown Honolulu. However, there are other things to see and do on Oahu that you should not miss.

No American should come to Hawaii without visiting Pearl Harbor. A tour of the *USS Arizona* memorial includes a brief movie and a short boat trip to the sunken ship, which suffered the greatest loss of life (1,177) in the attack on December 7, 1941, that brought the United States into World War II. In all, nine U.S. Navy ships were sunk that morning, and 21 more were seriously damaged; 2,350 people died, including 68 civilians, and another 1,178 were injured. The memorial to their sacrifice is very moving and memorable. Also worthy of your time at Pearl Harbor is the *USS Missouri,* aboard which the Japanese signed the articles of surrender on August 15, 1945, ending World War II.

The north side of Oahu is definitely worth a visit. The highlight is a stop at Sunset Beach with its famous Banzai Pipeline, where the unusually sharp, shallow reef just below the surface combines with the force of the open Pacific to create tubular waves up to 12 feet or more in diameter. These challenging conditions make this a great place to watch some of the world's best surfers.

Further to the east, the Polynesian Cultural Center provides an entertaining and educational window into seven of the varied cultures of Polynesia.

From the well-know gentle hula from Hawaii to the fast hip-shaking *otea* from Tahiti (my personal favorite), a visit will provide insights into Polynesian dances, customs and beliefs, as well as the remarkable navigational skills that enabled the Polynesians to travel thousands of miles across the ocean. I highly recommend this opportunity to see how these people lived and played.

We always schedule our Hawaiian trips so that we spend the day of our flight home on Oahu. Since flights to the mainland generally leave in the early evening, we catch an early flight to Honolulu from whatever island we're visiting. At the island airport, we check our bags all the way through to home, keeping only what we need for the day. Once we arrive in Honolulu, we rent a car and have six to eight hours to tour Oahu. The main road around the entire island is only about 80 miles, so you can cover a lot of ground in one day.

One of the prettiest and one of the saddest sights of our many visits to Hawaii is always the view of Diamond Head Crater on the plane's left side as we take off for home.

Whichever island you select as your main destination, I recommend booking a trip to Hawaii the next time you're looking for a relaxing vacation 'hat still offers plenty to see and do. And don't forget pack a copy of James Michener's *Hawaii* to read the flight over, if you haven't read it before. (I've it twice.)

Ve can't wait for our next visit to Hawaii. There) place like it in the world.

CHAPTER 42

LOOKING AHEAD

Another year has passed
and we're all a little older.
Last summer felt hotter
and winter seems much colder.

There was a time not long ago
when life was quite a blast.
Now I fully understand
About 'Living in the Past.'

We used to go to weddings,
football games and lunches.
Now we go to funeral homes,
and after-funeral brunches.

We used to have hangovers,
from parties that were gay.
Now we suffer body aches
and wile the night away.

We used to go out dining
and couldn)t get our fill.
Now we ask for doggie bags,
come home and take a pill.

We used to often travel
to places near and far.
Now we get sore asses
from riding in the car.

We used to go to nightclubs
and drink a little booze.
Now we stay home at night
and watch the evening news.

That, my friend is how life is
and now my tale is told.
So, enjoy each day and live it up...
before you're too damned old!

— Author unknown

I am writing this final chapter on the occasion of my 65th birthday. Coincidentally, the above poem was forwarded to me by my 89-year-old mother over the Internet just two days ago. I am not sure that the words capture my view of the future for me and my wife; but I am sure that the last two lines are very appropriate.

Although I expect that we have many good ʼ ahead of us, I can already see that the future ʼ different than the past. Both my wife and I ʼd excellent health until last year. Within the ʼonths I have had surgery to repair a hernia and a prostrate biopsy that, to my great relief, turned out clear. My wife fell and broke her wrist, requiring surgery to install a plate, then a second surgery to remove the plate. Now she is experiencing severe pain in one of her knees and may need a knee replacement.

It is obvious that after a certain age, things do not get better but begin to wear out. My mother has told me that getting old is not for sissies. A friend has said that staying alive requires staying active, and that requires hard work.

My current view (or hope) is that we will be able to continue to take two trips a year for at least ten more years. The focus for most of that travel will be in South America and Asia, although there are a few spots in Europe that we haven't visited yet.

We would like to see some different parts of the U.S. and Canada, also, but that can wait.

Based on the experiences of the guys I play golf with and others at my club, I should be able to golf for many years to come. I may have to start using the shorter teeing areas in a few years, but that won't impact the social or competitive nature of the game.

My parents are still doing pretty well at 93 and 89, so I am looking forward to keeping my schedule full for years to come.

Who knows? I may even write another book.

CPSIA information can be obtained
at www.ICGtesting.com
Printed in the USA
BVHW040934081219
565988BV00017B/909/P